WEAPON

THE LEE-ENFIELD RIFLE

MARTIN PEGLER

OSPREY PUBLISHING
Bloomsbury Publishing Plc

Kemp House, Chawley Park, Oxford OX2 9PH, UK
29 Earlsfort Terrace, Dublin 2, Ireland
1385 Broadway, 5th Floor, New York, NY 10018, USA
Email: info@ospreypublishing.com
www.ospreypublishing.com

OSPREY is a trademark of Osprey Publishing Ltd

First published in Great Britain in 2012
Transferred to digital print in 2023

A catalogue record for this book is available from the
British Library

Print ISBN: 978 1 84908 788 9
ePDF: 978 1 84908 789 6
ePub: 978 1 78096 034 0

Page layout by Mark Holt
Battlescene artwork by Peter Dennis
Index by Alan Thatcher
Typeset in Sabon and Univers
Originated by PDQ Digital Media Solutions, Suffolk, UK
Printed and bound in India by Replika Press Private Ltd.

24 25 26 27 20 19 18 17 16 15

Acknowledgements

I would like to thank a number of institutions and individuals
for their assistance. The collections of the Imperial War
Museum, National Army Museum, Australian War Memorial,
Canadian War Museum, National Firearms Museum, and
Royal Armouries have been invaluable. Several individuals have
provided photographs, in particular Peter Smith and Bob Maze.
My thanks also to the hard-working and long-suffering editorial
and production staff of Osprey, who turn the often imperfect
offerings of authors into the finished work that you see before
you. I do try hard to avoid making errors of fact, but any errors
or omissions are entirely mine.

Image acknowledgements
Cover images are courtesy of the National Firearms Museum
(NRAmuseum.com) and the Imperial War Museum
(IWM Q 3990).

Imperial War Museum Collections
Many of the photos in this book come from the Imperial War
Museum's huge collections which cover all aspects of conflict
involving Britain and the Commonwealth since the start of the
twentieth century. These rich resources are available online
to search, browse and buy at www.iwmcollections.org.uk. In
addition to Collections Online, you can visit the Visitor Rooms
where you can explore over 8 million photographs, thousands of
hours of moving images, the largest sound archive of its kind in
the world, thousands of diaries and letters written by people in
wartime, and a huge reference library. To make an appointment,
call (020) 7416 5320, or e-mail: mail@iwm.org.uk

Imperial War Museum www.iwm.org.uk

Artist's note

Readers may care to note that the original paintings from which
the colour plates in this book were prepared are available for
private sale. All reproduction copyright whatsoever is retained
by the Publishers. All enquiries should be addressed to:

Peter Dennis, 'Fieldhead', The Park,
Mansfield, Nottinghamshire NG18 2AT, UK

Email: magie.h@ntlworld.com

The Publishers regret that they can enter into no correspondence
upon this matter.

The Woodland Trust
Osprey Publishing supports the Woodland Trust, the UK's
leading woodland conservation charity.

www.ospreypublishing.com
To find out more about our authors and books visit our website.
Here you will find extracts, author interviews, details of
forthcoming events and the option to sign-up for our newsletter.

CONTENTS

INTRODUCTION

There are few rifles as immediately recognizable as the No. 1 Mk III Short, Magazine Lee-Enfield (SMLE). Service rifles seldom had nicknames bestowed on them; the generic 'bundook' (from *bundhook*, the Hindustani word for a rifle) was commonly used in the 19th and early 20th centuries, but the Mk III Lee-Enfield was one of very few modern rifles to earn an affectionate name, that of the 'Smellie'. The pugnacious muzzle with its jutting bayonet boss and distinctive protective wings on the fore- and rearsights give it an appearance unlike that of any other military rifle of its time, and it has subsequently become an iconic symbol, particularly of World War I.

Yet the Mk III was only one of 13 Enfield models adopted throughout the course of its service life. (This figure covers only the official patterns, not modified rifles such as the Mk I*.) Its initial introduction came in the guise of the Lee-Metford, which had an approval date of 22 December 1888; its full title was announced as Rifle, Magazine Lee-Metford Mk 8, August 1891. From 1888, therefore, until finally taken out of service, the Lee-Enfield served the British and Commonwealth armies for slightly less than 100 years. Although as a service rifle it was replaced by the FN/FAL in the British Army in 1957, the sniper variant, the L42A1, was to continue in use until supplanted by the Accuracy International L96A1 rifle in 1982. The Lee-Enfield saw combat through two world wars and a host of lesser conflicts, and it has been used in every conceivable theatre of war, from the trenches of World War I to the bitter cold of Norway in 1940, and from the blazing deserts of the Middle East to the jungles of Burma. It was carried by Allied troops in its millions and its high build quality and tough construction made it all but indestructible. It has long been regarded as militarily obsolete, yet examples are still found across the world being carried by irregular troops, police, militia and insurgents. Lee-Enfields are often recovered in Afghanistan, where they have been used against Coalition soldiers. News footage today frequently shows Third World soldiers carrying assorted models of the Lee-Enfield and the readily available supply of spare parts means that they are unlikely to vanish for some time yet. Indeed, so popular is the marque that there are now several companies manufacturing replacement parts.

Exactly how the Lee-Enfield came into being is a fascinating and sometimes complex story. It occurred, quite fortunately, at a time when the British Army was looking for a new and modern rifle design to replace the single-shot Martini-Henry with its outmoded falling-block action (this was a simple breech-block that was raised or lowered by means of a lever beneath the trigger – strong, reliable but slow to operate). The net result was a new rifle whose development was not simply the result of a drawing-board exercise at the Royal Small Arms Factory (RSAF) at Enfield Lock, but in fact owed much to the success of a number of existing designs of magazine bolt-action rifles. Its introduction was not without problems and it had many detractors, but it proved to be the most reliable and enduring of British service rifles and was, uniquely, issued as a single model to all branches of the armed services.

Four men of 2nd Battalion, The Gordon Highlanders, cautiously advance through a village in northern France, late 1944. Two, with fixed bayonets on their No. 4 rifles, cover the rear, while the others watch for enemy snipers. (IWM B 14608)

DEVELOPMENT
Trials and tribulations

In 1871 the British Army was re-equipped with the reliable single-shot .450in Martini-Henry rifle, which had replaced the stop-gap breech-loading Snider in service since 1866. The Martini was regarded as something of a milestone in weapon design and production when first introduced, but by the mid-1870s magazine-fed rifles were becoming available, although there were design limitations imposed because of the primitive ammunition. Black-powder-loaded cartridges were generally big, their large bullets requiring an equally large charge, and attempting to magazine-feed these cartridges was problematic. In addition, the cartridge bodies were made of brass foil and the rifle extractor had a distressing habit of tearing the riveted steel base off during extraction, leaving the body of the case jammed in the breech. They were also slow to reload, but at least that prevented, in the minds of the Board of Ordnance, the wanton wastage of ammunition by the soldiery that would result from introducing a faster-firing mechanism. The Martini-Henry was a well-designed and soldier-proof weapon, successful enough to be considered for possible modification to use an improved cartridge, the smaller .402in, which could be fed by means of a side-mounted magazine. It may well have been introduced as the next rifle for general service had not events in Europe caused a drastic re-evaluation by the Board in the mid-1880s.

What changed the Board's collective mind was the emergence in 1884 of a smokeless propellant called pyrocellulose (nitrocellulose as it is now known), a chemical formula perfected by a French chemist named Paul Vieille. The new powder burned hotter and faster than black powder, resulting in higher pressure and faster velocity, and enabling bullet diameters to be much reduced. Crucially, it did not create the awful corrosive fouling of gunpowder or expose the shooter's position by creating a pall of white smoke. It would be a slight exaggeration to say that black powder became obsolete overnight, but with the introduction of nitro powder its use in Europe dwindled very rapidly and smokeless propellants had become predominant within a couple of years, which was, by any standards, a very short timescale indeed.

Several individuals were to contribute materially to the eventual success of the Lee-Enfield rifles, and one of the most significant was William Metford. Born in Taunton in 1824, Metford inherited his love of firearms from his doctor father and in 1840 became an engineering apprentice for the Wiltshire, Somerset & Weymouth Railway. Metford was particularly intrigued by ballistics and bullet design, and for target use he produced ammunition that was renowned for its accuracy. (He did not patent it, and it is highly probable that Joseph Whitworth later pirated the design for use in his rifles.) But it was his work on barrel rifling that was to prove one of the most crucial elements in the development of the Lee-Enfield rifles. He believed, with justification, that the use of smaller-calibre bullets was more efficient than the traditional large lead types. He created a barrel with shallow seven-groove left-hand twist rifling that proved extremely stable for black-powder loaded ammunition, and when mated to the experimental .402in bullet it seemed that an ideal compromise had been reached. Indeed, the introduction of a new .402in Martini-Metford rifle was seen by many as almost a foregone conclusion.

Working in parallel with Metford was another brilliant engineer, a Scot named James Paris Lee, born in Hawick in 1831. Having made his own gun at the age of 12, Lee became happily obsessed with firearms and explosives for the rest of his life, despite accidentally shooting himself twice, and blowing himself up with a gunpowder charge that put him in hospital for 18 months. He surprised his family by actually reaching adulthood and it was fortunate that he did so, for his later work would prove vital in the development of the modern rifle. He initially became an apprentice clock-maker, but moved to Ontario in Canada at the age of 18,

Propellants: left to right, black powder, cordite and nitrocellulose. (Author)

then on to Wisconsin in the USA in 1858. By this time he had achieved some modest success as a firearms designer. He felt that the future of small-arms design lay in a combination of breech-loading and repeating fire using magazines, so he began to experiment with breech-loading conversions of existing rifles. His Springfield rifle conversion was very efficient, and during the American Civil War he received an order for 1,000, which unfortunately for him coincided with the end of the conflict.

At the same time, Lee was trying to perfect a more sophisticated pattern of rifle, in which multiple cartridges could be stored and fired as fast as they could be loaded. A modified Martini-Henry with side-mounted magazine worked tolerably well, being capable of firing 28 rounds per minute (rpm), but chambering and ejecting the cartridges proved awkward with the Martini's falling-block action. Lee's genius was in producing a magazine that fitted underneath the receiver body, in which the cartridges were stacked vertically on top of a feed plate that had a Z-shaped spring underneath it. This design meant that the magazine could only be reloaded when it was detached, but Lee suggested that spare loaded magazines could be carried for quick replacement. Ever mindful of the concerns the Army had over ammunition wastage, he stressed that these magazines could be loaded with one round at a time if so required, or removed totally (thereby negating the whole purpose of magazine loading). In 1876 Lee introduced his rotating-bolt (turnbolt) rifle, although this was not by any means the first of its type. In the USA the Ward-Burton had been issued in 1871, the Merrill-Brown in 1872 and the Hotchkiss in 1878. However, the Lee design was both simple and strong, and was extremely influential in shaping the design of the later family of Enfield rifles.

While in London in 1879, Colonel Frank Hyde of the Sharps Rifle Company – then the manufacturer of the Lee design – presented a Lee Model 1879 rifle to the Small Arms Committee (SAC) of the War Office for testing. Britain was keen to upgrade its existing Martini-Henry service rifle, and in March 1880 exhaustive testing was begun with nine models. These were: the Gardner rifle; the Green rifle; the Hotchkiss Model 1880 rifle; the Kropatschek system rifle; the Lee Model 1879 rifle; the Lee carbine; the Winchester Model 1876 rifle; the Vetterli Model 1878 rifle; and the Mauser Model 1871 modified with Lee-pattern magazine.

The committee disliked tube magazines, reasoning that they were potentially dangerous, as the nose of each bullet rested on the primer of the cartridge in front. This attitude was reinforced after Private G. Gregory of The Royal Welsh Fusiliers was badly injured when a cartridge in the Winchester detonated in the magazine during testing. Three models – the Hotchkiss, Winchester and Kropatschek – were immediately eliminated and never again were tube magazines considered for British military

service. After considerable testing, the Model 1879 Lee, Mauser and Green were regarded as potentially worthy of future trials, but there were some reservations about the Lee:

> The parts seem strong and easy to manufacture [but] the action of the extractor is not satisfactory … chiefly due to the form of the extractor. The action … is so arranged as to compress the mainspring at the same time as the cartridge is pushed into the chamber. This is a disadvantage as the force necessary to compress the spring entirely prevents feeding the cartridge into the chamber … it is essential that it should be felt and withdrawn instead of being driven home … which is liable to cause premature explosion before the bolt is locked.[1]

In other words, the mainspring was far too strong, and in the event of a fired cartridge sticking in the breech it was possible (although highly unlikely) that a fresh round could be detonated without being properly chambered. Notwithstanding this, it was felt that the Lee had sufficient merit to be worthy of further examination. The bolt design of the Lee cocked the striker as the bolt was closed, whereas the Mauser cocked on opening. In addition, the locking lug system was at the rear of the bolt and while some believed it to be less strong than the Mauser, it was certainly faster to operate. Unfortunately the Lee was chambered for the .45in Springfield cartridge, which was not a British service calibre, so the staff at the RSAF Enfield requested permission to convert it to .45in Gatling by the simple expedient of putting a Henry barrel into it and modifying several internal parts; this weapon was subsequently known as the Improved Model of 1882.

In spring 1883, another Lee was delivered to the RSAF Enfield for trials. This was a Model 1882 Remington-Lee, Remington by now having been contracted to manufacture the rifles. It was tested against an Owen-Jones falling-block rifle and another Lee fitted with a Bethel Burton external magazine. The Model 1882 acquitted itself very well, the SAC report of 1884 stating that 'This rifle is fitted with a simple and strong bolt action and differs from most bolt guns in having a powerful extraction, the original mechanism having been improved at the RSAF. The components of the breech-action are few in number, are easily manufactured, and are not liable to become unserviceable from use.'[2] The Committee also liked the fact that the magazine was detachable, stating that 'The magazine … is carried filled on the person of the soldier and is only attached to the rifle when required. The magazine must be removed from the rifle for the purpose of recharging it.'[3] A magazine cut-off was fitted to the left side of the rifle to prevent 'unwarranted expenditure of the ammunition'.[4] The cut-off served to turn the rifle into a single-shot weapon when the magazine was detached.

New Zealand troops occupy a breastwork trench in the Armentières sector of the Western Front, June 1916. The man second from left is aiming a periscope rifle while a spotter watches through a trench periscope. Their relaxed demeanour indicates a posed photograph, taken while out of immediate danger. (IWM Q 666)

The rifle was found to be quick to load and shoot – 5.6 seconds for six rounds and 22.3 seconds for ten rounds – and the accuracy of the .45in bullet was considered acceptable for military purposes, being capable of grouping a little over 2in at 100yd and achieving an 8in group at 500yd. Nothing was ever rushed where military trials were concerned, though, and the president of SAC requested that further exhaustive tests be undertaken in November 1886, between the two front-runners, the Owen-Jones and an RSAF-modified .402in Lee. These were tested, not by the Army but by the Royal Navy at HMS *Excellent*, the Portsmouth-based weapons testing and training establishment. The Navy were nothing if not thorough, and their report of December 1886 stated in précis that, of the two models:

> The Lee was of much greater simplicity of construction and less likely to get out of order. Spare parts were much more easily replaced ... the Lee-Burton magazine was much more simple and easily detached, the Lee extractor more powerful ... and ... the bolt action was preferred over the block due to its shorter movement: the falling block had the disadvantage of carrying dust or wet into the rifle when the block was lowered.[5]

But still no decision was made, for there had been two new arrivals in the firearms marketplace, the Rubini and Schulhof rifles. Both of these weapons were equipped with side-mounted hopper magazines and had bolt-action mechanisms, so SAC delayed its decision until they too had been tested. In some ways this delay was to the benefit of Lee, for an improved Model 1886 Remington-Lee with detachable box magazine was by then available, and an example of this latest rifle was provided for test in mid-January 1887. Bolt design was simplified to facilitate disassembly[6] and the cut-off was now situated on the right side. Perhaps of greater importance to SAC was the new design of five-round box magazine, mounted underneath the receiver. The initial trials rifles had magazines that required them to be removed prior to loading, but the new model could be loaded in situ, through the top of the receiver. Several were fitted with the new Speed patent magazine cut-off device, which enabled a full magazine to be isolated by sliding a steel plate across the top, while still allowing single rounds to be fired.[7] (J.J. Speed was the manager of the RSAF at Enfield from 1891 to 1909; he took out a number of useful patents, but never received any monetary reward from the War Office for them.) The rifle was chambered for the 11mm or .43in Spanish cartridge and was the final model supplied to SAC (that model is now in the collection of the Royal Armouries).

In a lecture at the Royal United Services Institute (RUSI) in the summer of 1887, Major-General Bray of the SAC outlined the main dilemma facing the committee in making the right choice:

The Remington Lee is a splendid weapon; it has a magazine underneath which contains six [sic] cartridges, it has a beautiful barrel, and is an admirable weapon, having this advantage: the captain of the company can control the magazine fire. The ... soldier ... recovers the arm at the word 'Magazine load'. It is done in an instant. Then he can also give the order 'Magazine unload' so that he controls the fire of his company. Whereas if the cartridges are in the barrel of the gun, or in the magazines under the entire control of the soldier, when once you get into action you will find it almost impossible to control the fire of your men. There are two views to take of a rifle – the accurate fire question and the military efficiency question, and they are as distinct as two things can well be from each other. The theoretical men are all for putting on bull's eyes at 1,000 yards [914m], the practical men are for putting a rifle in the hands of the British soldier with which he can shoot down his enemy at distances under 400 yards [366m], those important points must never be separated.[8]

A nice picture of a typical early-World War I Regular soldier wearing full marching order. His Mk I SMLE has the Pattern 1907 bayonet fitted, still with its troublesome hooked quillon. (Peter Smith)

That this new rifle met with approval is evidenced in the final SAC report, which recommended the adoption of the Lee action and magazine system, with a few caveats, namely that the best form of rifling be decided on, the bolt be improved and a suitable cartridge adopted. The first two problems were fairly easily solved: seven-groove Metford rifling was believed to be the most efficient and modification to the bolt-locking system was undertaken. Some 350 Model 1888 Lee Trials rifles were to be manufactured at Enfield, provisionally called the '.303 Pattern Magazine Trials rifle, 1888' and 50 carbines (eventually 387 rifles and 51 carbines were completed). These were considerably improved over the previous Lee models, incorporating a large number of modifications, such as: a pivoting bolt-head, which could be replaced easily to ensure correct cartridge head-spacing; a thumb-latch on the cocking piece of the bolt; a longer ejector; strengthened body; reduced magazine dimensions (the magazine was held by a small chain to prevent loss); a butt trap for oil and cleaning jag; a cleaning rod; and a modified bayonet lug for a new pattern of knife bayonet, the Pattern 1888. All that was left now was further testing in order to determine exactly what the optimal calibre and charge should be.

EARLY CARTRIDGE DEVELOPMENT

The US government .45-70in ammunition used in the Lee Model 1879 rifles was never adopted by the British Army, so the improved model chambering the .45in Gatling was simply a stopgap measure, and the Remington Lee models supplied in 1886 had all been adapted for the proposed new .402in cartridge. The rifle could well have been adopted at this point in the new calibre, but Vieille's introduction of smokeless propellant and its inordinately rapid adoption by the French Army as the Modèle 1886 Lebel 8mm rifle rendered obsolete all previous experimental work with black-powder ammunition. Suddenly, small-calibre, high-velocity rounds were *de rigeur* and governments around the world were caught up in the rush to adopt this new ammunition.

It could not have come at a more awkward time for Britain; having invested so much time and money in developing the new .402in round, it was faced with having to change course mid-stream. However, one of the surprise results that had come from the earlier rifle testing was the performance of one of the rifles, or rather its cartridge. The Model 1889 Swiss Rubin chambered a 7.5×53mm rimless cartridge and its performance was excellent. With a 130-grain paper-patched bullet (the bullet was wrapped in a thin layer of paper to seal the bore and prevent lead stripping against this rifling) it achieved a heady 3,000ft/sec (914m/sec); even with heavier 174-grain military ball, it produced an impressive 2,560ft/sec (780m/sec), giving it an effective range in excess of 1,500yd (1,371m) with greater energy and flatter trajectory than any contemporary black-powder load. The design of the Rubin cartridge was regarded by Britain as difficult for mass production. Its rimless, acute bottlenecked design was disliked by SAC, who believed it was prone to jamming as well as being difficult for

The primary marks of .303in cartridges, with their dates of introduction in brackets. From left: S.A. Ball Mk I, black powder propellant (1891); S.A. Ball Mk IIC, cordite propellant (1893); S.A. Ball Mk VIIC, cordite, pointed bullet (1911); S.A. Ball Mk VIIZ, nitrocellulose charge, for machine-gun use (1917); S.A. Ball, Mk VIIIZ (1939), the last pattern of .303in cartridge, loaded with Neonite, a nitrocellulose-based propellant. (Author)

chambering in machine guns. It was also felt to be likely to snag on the rim of the preceding cartridge. The bullet was therefore altered to .303in (actually .312in) and while a semi-rimless design performed excellently, the superintendent of RSAF was so opposed to it that it was abandoned in favour of a fully rimmed case, which was manufactured by Royal Laboratories, Woolwich. The new cartridge was finally adopted on 2 February 1889, as the 'Cartridge, S.A. Ball .303 inch Powder, Mk I'. At this point, it was determined that all military ammunition be date- and manufacturer-marked by means of stampings on the base, so that any batch that proved faulty could be traced, a practice that continues in both commercial and military ammunition manufacturing to this day.

The .303in was in many respects already an old-fashioned design, with its rimmed, tapered, bottlenecked body and round-nosed bullet, for most nations had opted for rimless cases and pointed bullets. Oddly too, in view of the global change that had taken place with the adoption of smokeless powder, the new ammunition was to be loaded with black powder. In fairness, SAC stated that this was to be a temporary measure, as it was felt that within the available timeframe for adoption of the new rifle a suitable smokeless cartridge could not be properly designed and tested. The Mk I cartridge was, in fact, replaced by a cordite-loaded one in early 1892, whereupon the 1,600yd graduations on the rearsights had to be replaced by new 1,800yd settings, and this was to cause some accuracy problems when used in combat. As the rifles began to see limited general issue, one unforeseen shortcoming emerged when it was found that upon firing, some bullets were leaving their metal jacket casings behind in the barrel, the lead core being blown through by the pressure of the explosion. As a result, the projectile was modified with a thicker jacket and a Mk II bullet introduced.

THE MAGAZINE LEE-METFORD RIFLES

Even if the type of propellant could not be settled upon, deciding on the calibre had been a positive move forwards, and in the List of Changes (the official publication announcing the acceptance of a new model, marque or type of military weapon or piece of equipment) for 1 December 1889 the adoption of a new service rifle was announced, the 'Magazine Rifle, Mark I', generally known as the Lee-Metford. In fact, by that date it was already under production at government manufactories at Enfield, as well as by Birmingham Small Arms (BSA) at Sparkbrook and Small Heath, and by London Small Arms (LSA) at Old Ford in London. It differed from the previous incarnation in several significant respects. The raised thumb-piece on the rear of the trials rifle was superfluous (and it required 32 machining operations) and Lewes sights were fitted (see below for description). The bolt could now be carried at half-cock and had a distinctive sheet-steel dust cover and also a safety catch. A wooden top-guard was fitted with finger grooves beneath, and the stock was two-piece, with a butt available in long and short configurations.

The unusual flip-up long-range rearsight on a Magazine Lee-Metford Mk II. This design of rearsight was retained on the SMLE Mk I. (National Firearms Museum, NRAmuseum.com)

The rearsight was particularly unusual in having a normal ladder-type sight, now graduated to 1,900yd (1,737m), but additionally a long-range (or volley) sight was placed on the left side of the body. This odd arrangement in theory enabled a soldier to aim from 1,800yd to 3,500yd (1,646–3,200m) by raising the rotating front sight to register the required distance, then peering through the offset rear sight. As no human target would be visible to the human eye at such distances, the practicality of the arrangement on a modern rifle was questionable, but it did prove of use at times where massed targets were visible at long range, and it was to survive for many years. The barrel was now a Metford seven-groove of 30.2in (774mm) length with left-hand twist of one turn in 10in (.33in calibre). The capacity of the box magazine was reduced from ten to eight rounds in a single stack.

The Mk I was a complex rifle to make, requiring 950 separate machining operations on 88 individual parts. The initial commercial price of the rifle was £5 16s each – using average earnings as a base this equates today to £465 (all values have been calculated using the Retail Price Index to give an approximate comparison of purchasing power). Colonel Slade of SAC enthused over it, writing that:

> No arm that has come before the SAC combines so many of the essentials of a military rifle as the one about to be introduced into our service. It is strong and handy and of convenient weight. The accuracy leaves nothing to be desired, the absolute mean deviation at 1000 yards [914m] being a little over one foot [305mm]. The trajectory of the bullet is low and there is no recoil perceptible. As regards the magazine it is strong and simple, difficult to injure, and easy to repair, or capable of being replaced by a spare one.[9]

Even allowing for some hyperbole, there was little doubt that the new rifle was a huge step forwards and ensured that the British Army's soldiers were carrying a state-of-the-art weapon. Some 13,000 had been made by the end of 1889 and these were issued to line regiments for field trials. In addition to the manufacture of the long rifle, a cavalry carbine variant

TOP
A Magazine Lee-Metford Mk II rifle, made by BSA Sparkbrook. (National Firearms Museum, NRAmuseum.com)

BOTTOM
The Mk I Lee-Metford cavalry carbine was nearly 10in shorter than the rifle and fitted with a six-round magazine. (© Board of Trustees of the Armouries; ex-MoD Pattern Room Collection)

was also designed, and this compact weapon (the Magazine Lee-Metford Carbine Mk I) was to be functionally identical but almost 10in (254mm) shorter, with a six-round magazine. Its rearsight was optimistically graduated to 2,000yd (1,829m), and it was 2lb 1oz (0.9kg) lighter. In total some 13,479 were manufactured before the model was phased out with the introduction of the new short rifle.

Aside from the problem mentioned with the black-powder ammunition, the new rifle generally performed well. There were some difficulties with the pattern of sights fitted, specifically the curiously notched Lewes foresight, which proved poor; it was replaced by a more standard barleycorn foresight, and the graduation on the long-range sight was reduced to 2,900yd (2,652m). Lesser improvements were made with firing and magazine springs, and a brass butt disc was introduced onto which regimental markings could be stamped. Curiously, the safety catch was omitted as well, and the nomenclature of the rifle was officially changed on 9 January 1892 to 'Magazine Rifle, Lee-Metford Mk I Improved (M.L.M.Mk I*)'.

The development process continued unabated, however, and within a short space of time a Mk II was proposed, incorporating some 42 modifications, of which arguably the most significant was an improved magazine holding ten rounds in two columns, and a thumb-operated safety catch was added to the rear right of the bolt. The finger grooves were omitted and yet more alterations were made to the rearsight and long-range sight. The method of fixing the bayonet was improved, although the same Pattern 1888 bayonet was used. The brass disc vanished from these rifles, as they had a long tang on the buttplate onto which regimental markings were stamped. The final approval was announced in the List of Changes of 12 April 1893 (List of Changes approval dates were 30 January 1892 and 12 April 1893). To allow for the now-general issue of smokeless powder, the depth of rifling was increased and it was decided that the contract for 200,000 rifles currently under production should incorporate as many Mk II features as possible, so approximately half were made to the new specifications. Volume production costs dropped too, trade retail price being £4 for the Mk I* and £5 for the Mk II (£338 and £442 respectively at today's prices). A Mk II* was introduced and is recognizable by the thumb-safety lever fitted to the right side of the bolt just behind the cocking handle.

Despite all of the improvements and the considerable costs incurred in modification, the Lee-Metford was still widely regarded in many quarters with suspicion, however. There was also a huge cost implication in manufacturing and issuing two patterns – carbines and rifles – the former being inaccurate at longer ranges and the latter still proving to have a number of defects. There were problems with barrel wear and resultant poor accuracy, plus vulnerable

The ineffectual and unpopular Lewes front sight with its odd foresight notch, instead of the more practical blade. (Bob Maze)

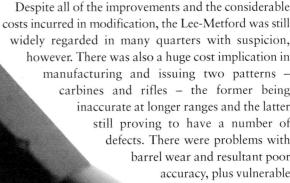

Commercial adverts for the Lee-Enfields, from a magazine of 1912. (Bob Maze)

sights and difficulties in loading ammunition due to awkward magazine access. The length and weight of the rifle were also troublesome, as was the bayonet fitting. These issues prompted SAC to call for yet further experimentation to produce a revised model.

THE MAGAZINE LEE-ENFIELDS

Still unhappy with the Lee-Metford design, SAC proposed yet another revision of the model to try to remedy all of the major shortcomings of the Mk II rifle. Current Mauser Model 1895s were examined for comparison, these being the largest-selling bolt-action rifles then available and the ones most often faced by British soldiers throughout the Second Boer War (1899–1902). There were concerns, too, over the lack of longevity of the Metford rifling when used with the new, hotter cordite ammunition. Work continued on trying to find a successful compromise between the long and carbine patterns, as well as ironing out the niggling problems that persisted.

The net result of this was the introduction of two Magazine Rifles, Lee-Enfield Mk I (11 November 1895) and Mk I* (19 May 1899), which had been fitted with Enfield-made five-groove barrels that retained the same twist rate. Small changes were also made during this period; for the first time the clearing rod was abolished in British service and, inevitably it seemed, the graduations of the rearsight changed, with the Mk I* having a folding leaf rearsight graduated from 200yd to 2,000yd (182–1,828m).

Many of these rifles also had the circular butt-disc fitted to them and in total some 42,000 were manufactured. Subsequently many were further converted to charger-loading, although there seems to be no official date for this; possibly they were modified as and when armourers were able to undertake the work. Certainly many appear in photographs of World War I, for although of older pattern, they proved good serviceable weapons.

THE SHORT, MAGAZINE LEE-ENFIELDS

SAC seemed to have become almost obsessed with creating the perfect rifle, and towards the latter half of 1901 it seemed that the solution may finally have been found. Some 1,055 'Shortened Enfield Modified Rifles' had been made at Enfield and sent for troop trials. The new rifle incorporated a host of detail changes: these included a fully enclosing top hand-guard along the barrel and two patterns of improved rearsight, 'A' and 'B', of which the former, graduated from 200yd to 2,000yd (183–1,829m), was eventually selected. Distinctive winged protectors were fitted behind the rearsight bed and the straight-blade foresight was similarly equipped with the addition of a novel and highly distinctive one-piece steel forend, which both protected the sight and provided a secure boss and lug fitment for the bayonet. Most significant of all, the rifle was reduced in length by no less than 5in (127mm) and its weight by 1lb 4oz (0.56kg), making it only 4.5in (114mm) longer than the Metford and Enfield cavalry carbines.

The quality of manufacture and detail of these rifles was exquisite: ivory knobs were fitted to the rearsight slide and fine adjustment provided for elevation and windage. A modified pattern was sent for testing in mid-December 1902, incorporating no fewer than 72 alterations from the Long Lee-Enfield that preceded it. It was accepted for service later that month (published in the List of Changes, 23 December 1902) as 'The Short, Magazine Lee-Enfield Rifle Mk I'. It is perhaps worth noting that over the years, the comma after 'Short' has often been abandoned and many firearms enthusiasts now believe that the nomenclature refers to a shortened magazine, whereas it simply refers to the reduced barrel length of the new rifle. Many units participated in the trials of 1902, including line regiments, cavalry, Royal Navy and marine units. Although there were some minor complaints, one persistent problem arose – that of poor accuracy on some rifles – the reason for which could not immediately be determined.

Speeding up the loading process was also regarded as a major issue, and after 1902 the first charger-loading Lee-Enfields were produced, with five-round clips supplied for faster charging. To enable these to function properly, the rifles were modified with the addition of a charger guide attached to the left side of the receiver and the retrofitting of a new bolt-head with a sliding charger guide; as a result the distinctive steel bolt dust cover was now omitted. Wear in the bolt-head charger guides resulted in a steel charger bridge being fitted above the receiver, and this was to become a permanent feature on all future Enfield models. A lever safety catch was fitted to the rear left receiver.

The distinctive blunt snout of the SMLE, showing the foresight protector and the very strong method of fixing the bayonet. (Author)

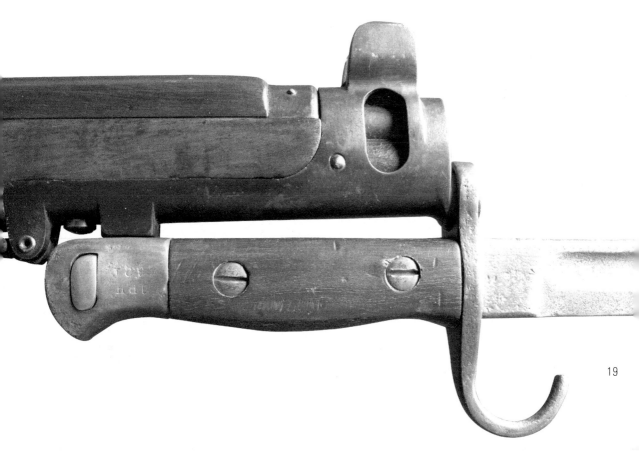

These changes were just the beginning, though, for attempts to find and correct the shortcomings with accuracy continued unabated. Experimentation in 1904 at Enfield with different barrel types showed that a short lead from the chamber into the barrel, allied to the adoption of a new form of Metford/Enfield rifling, improved matters greatly. The rifling modification required increasing the rifling twist towards the muzzle, a configuration known as progressive rifling. It enhanced performance by speeding up the rate of spin on the bullet and helping stabilize it, but did not entirely solve the matter. Eventually a bore with parallel but deeper rifling was introduced, but the two types co-existed until almost the end of World War I.

Another immediate problem in introducing a shorter barrel had been a slight drop in muzzle velocity to below 2,000ft/sec (610m/sec), and the barrel modifications helped to raise the performance back to an acceptable 2,200ft/sec (671m/sec). (A full performance table for the .303in cartridge is given on page 25.)

As a result of the testing, endless reports and recommendations, the sealed patterns for the SMLE Mk I and Mk II rifles were approved on 26 September 1906 and began to be introduced for service on 26 January the following year as the 'Rifle, Short, M.L.E. No. 1 Mark III'. As was

SMLE No. 1 Mk III parts drawing, from *The Service Rifle and How to Use It*

1	Blade foresight	**20**	Bolt head tenon	**41c**	Magazine auxiliary spring
2	Foresight block	**21**	Cocking-piece locking recess	**42**	Guard trigger
3	Band foresight block	**22**	Locking bolt	**43**	Stock forend
4	Key foresight block	**23**	Locking bolt flat	**44**	Spring and stud forend
5	Crosspin foresight block	**24**	Locking bolt thumbpiece	**45**	Rearsight protector
5a	Rearsight bed	**25**	Locking bolt aperture sight stem	**46**	Hand-guard front and rear
6	Rearsight bed crosspin	**26**	Locking bolt stop pin recess	**47**	Spring hand-guard rear
6a	Rearsight bed sight spring screw	**27**	Locking bolt safety catch stem	**48**	Lower band groove
7	Rearsight leaf	**28**	Locking bolt safety catch arm	**49**	Lower band
8	Rearsight slide	**29**	Locking bolt screw threads	**50**	Nosecap
9	Rearsight slide catch	**30**	Locking bolt seating	**51**	Foresight protector
10	Rearsight fine adjustment worm wheel	**31**	Bolt cam grooves	**52**	Sword bar
		32	Sear	**53**	Boss for ring of sword bayonet crosspiece
10a	Windgauge	**33**	Sear seating		
10b	Windgauge screw	**34**	Sear spring	**54**	Swivel seating
11	Rearsight ramps	**35**	Magazine catch	**55**	Swivel piling
12	Seating for safety catch	**36**	Full bent of cocking piece	**56**	Nosecap barrel opening
13	Safety catch	**37**	Short arm of sear	**57**	Inner band
14	Locking bolt stem	**38**	Trigger rib	**58**	Inner band screw
15	Bolt	**39**	Trigger rib	**59**	Inner band screw spring
16	Bolt head	**40**	Trigger	**60**	Butt sling swivel
17	Striker	**41**	Trigger axis pin	**61**	Sword bayonet, Pattern 1907
18	Cocking piece	**41a**	Magazine case	**62**	Bridge charger guide
19	Striker collar with stud	**41b**	Magazine platform spring	**63**	Cut-off

SHORT RIFLE, MAGAZINE LEE-ENFIELD (MARK III).

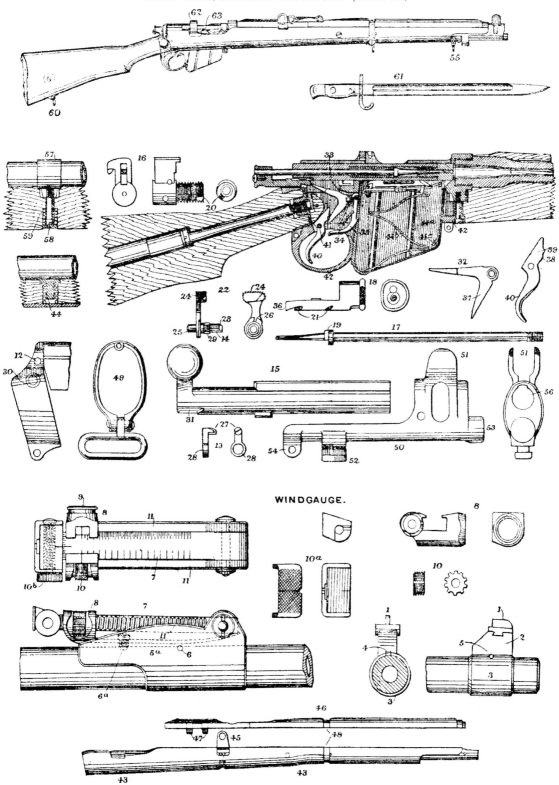

WINDGAUGE.

inevitably the case, the number of amendments and design modifications to the previous Mk I and Mk II were legion and space requirements make it impractical to reproduce a full list, but the rifle that was to become the most famous and recognizable long-arm in British military service had at last taken on its final form.

In précis, the SMLE was manufactured to very fine tolerances and all parts were interchangeable, with the exception of bolts (which required individual headspacing) and the forend and nosecap, which were serial numbered to each rifle to ensure barrel bedding and accuracy were not compromised. Most other parts were improved in some manner; there were differing blade heights for the foresight to allow for the use of the new Mk VI and Mk VII ammunition. The round-nosed Mk VI was introduced in 1904 but phased out with the introduction of the pointed Mk VII in 1911. The rearsight was given a U-notch and was adjustable to 2,000yd (1,829m) in 50yd (46m) increments, and fine windage adjustment was incorporated. Volley sights were still fitted to all rifles, graduated from 1,600yd to 2,800yd (1,463–2,560m). Tests at the School of Musketry at Hythe showed that, firing as fast as possible, 'experienced riflemen were able to load and fire up to an incredible sixty aimed shots per minute, far faster than any comparable service rifle. This with little or no loss of accuracy … targets at 300 yards [274m] being struck by all of the shots.'[10] Under more regulated conditions, a sergeant of The Rifle Brigade fired 25 aimed shots in one minute, all of which struck an 8×6in (203×153mm) target at 200yd (183m). Aside from the magazine capacity, this feat was made possible by the design of the bolt, with its short handle and angled lift, which was far more conducive to rapid fire without upsetting the aim.

The magazine was charger-loaded via the bridge over the receiver, and it held a useful ten rounds, 11 if the chamber was also loaded, more than any other military rifle then in service. The magazine cut-off was retained and the sheet-steel magazine itself was quickly detachable and easily field-stripped for cleaning. The bolt was removed for cleaning by pulling it to the rear and lifting the bolt-head up to unlock it from the receiver, which was accomplished in one short movement. The stock and woodwork were of

On the outbreak of war in 1914, many units, particularly Territorials, were still equipped with early-issue weapons and equipment. Here a young soldier of The Manchester Regiment carries an interesting modified charger-loading Lee-Enfield with finger-grooved stock and cut-out for the magazine cut-off. (Peter Smith)

With the introduction of the Short Rifle, the thumb safety visible here was removed and replaced by a sliding lever on the rear left of the receiver. This example of a charger-loading Mk I* Enfield saw service in World War I. (Bob Maze)

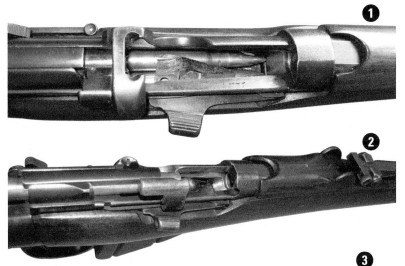

walnut, but were not easily disassembled, being designed for stripping only by a competent armourer. Stocks were available in two, then latterly three, lengths. The barrel retained its deeper Enfield rifling, with a 1-in-10, five-groove left-hand twist, and had to be manufactured to .3025in with no more or less than a 10 per cent deviation. Surprisingly, the adoption of this new rifle caused a huge furore at the time among both sporting and service shooters, and this row is covered more fully in the next chapter.

Use of a charger speeded up the loading process considerably. The cartridges were held in a sprung metal clip, usually five at a time, and the clip inserted into a guide at the rear of the receiver. When slotted into place, the cartridges were pushed by the thumb down into the magazine well, the clip removed and discarded and the process repeated. Ten cartridges could be loaded in as many seconds.

1. The magazine cut-off in closed position on a loaded magazine, demonstrating how the cartridges were retained. A single round could still be inserted into the breech. (Author)

2. Charger-loading required modifications to the rifle by fitting a fixed charger guide to the left of the receiver (visible at left centre) and a sliding charger guide to the bolt. The dust cover was dispensed with. In this picture, the bolt is half-retracted and the slot in the bolt head for the charger clip is just visible. (Bob Maze)

3. Clip of five rounds. (Author)

LATER AMMUNITION DEVELOPMENT

Cordite ammunition had been a great improvement over the old black-powder type. In 1911, a new cartridge – or to be more specific, a new bullet – was introduced, which was to become the standard for the remainder of the service life of the Enfield rifle. This was the 'Cartridge, S.A., Ball Mk VII, C', which used a cordite load but had a pointed, or spitzer, bullet. It delivered increased range and better stability, and like its predecessors the .303in bullet possessed tremendous penetrative power. An even more powerful round, the Mk VIIZ, was introduced in October 1917, using technology that had been adopted long before by the French and Germans. This had a pointed bullet, but also a tapered 'boat-tail' that streamlined it and provided extra range. It was primarily for use over longer ranges and an improved variant, the Mk VIIIZ, was introduced in 1939, mainly for aircraft and other machine-gun use. Although this ammunition could be used in service rifles, the greater chamber pressures generated did not make it a recommended practice. For snipers, there was never any special issue of ammunition – they used what they believed worked best; Herbert McBride, a highly experienced Canadian rifleman and sniper, commented that Winchester-made cartridges were particularly sought after. However, the armour-piercing cartridges approved for service in December 1915 (published in List of Changes, 1 February 1918) proved most acceptable to snipers, when and if they could obtain them.

In reality, the velocity and accuracy of the ammunition used in World War I was certainly more than adequate for the ranges involved. A Mk VII bullet fired from an SMLE could reach in excess of 2,000yd (1,829m), far beyond distances to which even a sniper could see. The performance of the .303in was roughly paralleled by other cartridges such as the German 7.92mm and French 8mm Lebel. The *Government Manual of Small Arms* (1911) stated that a .303in bullet at 200yd (183m) could penetrate 38in (965mm) of hardwood, 58in (1,470mm) of softwood, 14in (357mm) of lime-mortared brickwork, 18in (457mm) of packed sandbags and 60in (1,533mm) of clay-packed sandbags. A number of myths about modern high-velocity ammunition arose among the troops occupying the trenches, particularly within the ranks of the British Expeditionary Force (BEF), many of whom had fought in colonial wars where black-powder ammunition, with its relatively low velocities, was the norm. The Germans were accused of using dum-dum ammunition – bullets that had their noses filed down or snipped off to deliver more serious wounds (named after

During World War I, many regiments fought in France and Flanders with earlier-model rifles, and these men, who appear to be of The King's (Liverpool) Regiment, were photographed on the Somme in summer 1916. They hold charger-loading Mk I* Lee-Enfields, fitted with a mixture of leather and webbing slings. One wag (centre left) is also holding up a vital box of Woodbine cigarettes. (Author)

A collection of .303in bullets. From left: a Mk III/IV; the hollow-point Mk V (on its side), which was declared illegal under international law, and was replaced by (at centre) the pointed Mk VI; a standard 174-grain Mk VII; and the last pattern of .303in bullet, the 175-grain boat-tailed Mk VIIIZ. (Author)

the Dum Dum arsenal in India). Yet the men often simply failed to understand the terrible effects of close-range bullet strikes on the human body – and most trench shooting was characterized by its closeness, sometimes no more than 50yd (46m):

> I bandaged another chap whose arm, when in a horizontal position, had been hit by a bullet which shattered the whole forearm from wrist to elbow. My first-aid effort, I'm afraid was nothing more than parcelling up the pieces. The terrible injury caused by this one bullet made us wonder if Jerry was using dum-dum bullets. Later on we found several clips of German soft-nosed bullets, and, as opportunity offered, experienced grim satisfaction in shooting back with Mauser rifles.[11]

It should be noted that early German sniping rifles were often commercial hunting rifles adopted into military use, and they were chambered for the old 8mm Mauser cartridge. Many were used with commercial soft-nosed hunting ammunition.

Ammunition comparisons

.303in calibre

Nomenclature	Date	Filling	Bullet weight (grains)	Type*	Velocity (ft/sec)
Mk I/IIC	1889	BP	213	RN	2,000
Mk IC	1892	Cordite	215	RN	2,200
Mk II/IV	1897	Cordite	215	HP	2,200
Mk VIC	1904	Cordite	215	RN	2,300
Mk VII	1911	Cordite	174	S	2,750
Mk VIIZ	1917	Nitro	174	S	2,750
Mk VIIP	1917	Nitro	170	APS	2,750
Mk VIIIZ	1939	Nitro	175	SBT	2,900

7.62mm calibre

Nomenclature	Date	Filling	Bullet weight (grains)	Type*	Velocity (ft/sec)
Ball, L2A1/2	From 1970	Nitro	144	SBT	2,750

* RN: round nose; HP: hollow point; S: spitzer; APS: armour-piercing spitzer; SBT: boat-tailed spitzer.

In the wake of the war, questions began to be asked about the necessity for such powerful ammunition. After all, if a short-barrelled rifle was acceptable for general use, was there really any point in manufacturing bullets with ranges in excess of 2,000yd? That question was not to be addressed for another four decades.

WORLD WAR I PRODUCTION

The threat of war that hung heavily across Europe in the first decade of the 20th century did not go totally unnoticed by the British government, who were keen to increase rifle production as quickly as possible. BSA's output in the five years prior to 1914 had been a meagre 7,000 rifles (during the Second Boer War they were manufacturing 2,500 per week), production roughly parallel to that of Enfield, and even by 1914 total annual production of new rifles was only 108,000.[12] When it became clear that war was inevitable, production had to be significantly improved, so a supply chain known as the 'peddle scheme' was introduced. This scheme used a new organization, the Standard Small Arms Company (SSAC), which employed external contractors to provide screws, springs and other small items[13] – a system that had once been commonplace in the production of British muskets. This system provided a marked improvement in efficiency, leaving the three main factories (Enfield, BSA and LSA) to concentrate on major production items. As a result, production rose rapidly.

Even by today's standards such production figures are quite impressive, BSA calculating that they produced 1,310,000 components *a week* – this involved some 15,050,000 separate machining operations. Clearly, any

Not a Second Boer War photo, but a picture of British soldiers in a makeshift trench on Gallipoli. They have charger-loading Mk I Enfields, and the masks some wear over their faces are to give protection from dust rather than gas. (IWM Q 13404)

SMLE rifle production, 1914–18

Date	Number produced
August–December 1914	120,093 rifles
1915	613,461 rifles
1916	852,928 rifles
1917	1,205,572 rifles
1918	1,062,052 rifles[14]

reduction in the amount of machining would materially assist in speeding up production. From the figures in the chart, it can be seen that up to 1916 output had risen steadily but not spectacularly, but then it leapt to seven figures, partly as a result of the work done by the SSAC in improving supply via its chain of contractors, but also by reducing the manufacturing effort required by introducing the No. 1 Mk III* rifle on 2 January 1916.

This model was produced with a simplified bolt-head, no long-range sights or windage adjustment on the rearsight, and no magazine cut-off or front sling-swivel. The brass regimental butt-disc was once more omitted, although it is common to find examples of later-dated rifles that do not incorporate all of these modifications – some 1918-dated rifles have cut-offs, for example. The rigidity of inspection for some less critical parts was relaxed and wherever possible machining time was reduced (the barrel alone required 85 separate operations). By the end of the war, more than 29,000 rifles were being manufactured every day, and this did not include salvaged weapons that were returned for refurbishment. The price had dropped to £3 15s per unit (about £188 at today's value), a huge saving

Highlanders in occupied Germany, shifting apparently brand-new rifles and bayonets from a local railway station. The logistics of world war naturally demanded a massive increase in arms production, and in 1916 the SMLE was simplified to ease mass production – with the result that the pre-1916 rifles were arguably the last to be built to Victorian quality standards. (IWM Q 7543)

compared to the original 1888 price. With output at an all-time high, the cessation of hostilities in November 1918 brought rifle production to a sudden halt, but the ever-questioning minds of the members of SAC continued to work as hard as ever.

ADAPTATIONS, IMPROVEMENTS AND MODIFICATIONS

No one had predicted the emergence of trench warfare, and it is to the credit of its basic design that the Enfield coped admirably with the prevailing conditions. However, there had arisen a number of requirements that had never been considered by SAC, even in their wildest dreams. Undoubtedly the most significant, both during the war and afterwards, was the need for a telescopic-sight-equipped rifle to cope with the endless sniping that the Commonwealth soldiers faced. From the outset, many German soldiers had been trained and equipped for the role of sniping, but nothing existed in the British arsenal that was remotely capable of meeting this threat head-on. The story of how the British Army dealt with the threat is not relevant for this title, but at the core was the basic fact that whatever response was decided upon, the weapon of choice – the issue Lee-Enfield Mk III – was one that was never designed for the role of sniping.

There actually existed another rifle that could have been put to good use in the role, the Pattern 1914 Enfield. Produced for trials purposes in 1913, this Mauser-action weapon was originally designed for the advanced .276in high-velocity cartridge. Unfortunately wartime demand for the SMLE meant that the Pattern 1914 could not be manufactured in the UK, so it was produced under contract in the United States by Remington and Winchester in standard .303in calibre and latterly in .30in calibre for US service. Like its German counterpart, its design would have made it ideal for mounting a telescopic sight, but it was adopted too late to see service as a sniping rifle – it was not accepted into service until December 1918.

Despite their initial misgivings about the long-range accuracy of the SMLE, most target shooters had eventually adopted it, albeit in modified form. Fitted with heavy match barrels, specially bedded into their stocks, with lightened triggers (the Lee-Metford pulled at a hefty 8lb 8oz (3.9kg), about treble that of a match rifle) and aperture target sights, they were competent 1,000yd (914m) rifles. But such adaptations were expensive and time-consuming, so the decision of the Army Command to instigate a sniper training programme in early 1915 left the Army with the knotty problem of how to turn a rifle never designed for very accurate shooting into one that could accomplish just that.

The basic design of a Lee-Enfield, with its charger bridge over the receiver, meant that any form of mounting for a telescopic sight would block the charger guide. In practice, of course, the quickly detachable magazine meant that this mattered little, but the Army was insistent that any optical sight was mounted offset to the left, to enable charger clips and the iron sights to be used. The fact that snipers were seldom required single-handedly to beat off massed enemy attacks did not seem to occur to them. There was some attempt at standardization, with the introduction of Specification No. S.A. 390 in May 1915 for the production of sniper rifles and mounts, but there were insufficient manufacturers with the experience to design and fit telescopic sights and mounts properly.

As a result a rather bewildering number of variants appeared. Virtually all 9,778 Enfields[15] converted for sniper use had their mounts offset to the left, which made for uncomfortable shooting (using the left eye was generally easier, but not all men were able to do it) and placed the snipers at a disadvantage when using loophole plates, for angling the rifle to the right caused the firer's vision to be blocked. As one former sniper recalled, 'I saw a German walking casually behind [the trench], but by the time I had my telescope on him, he was too far to the right and I couldn't get a shot off at the bugger.'[16]

Despite using a similar charger system, the Germans had no difficulties with mounting optical sights above the receiver, understanding that snipers fired only when necessary and could remove their scopes when required. Nevertheless, the British and Commonwealth snipers soldiered on with a motley assortment of scopes and mounts, manufactured by at least 21 different companies. The Enfields proved to be competent but not outstanding sniping weapons, and it was perhaps fortunate that most

There were many sniping variants of the SMLE. This picture, taken in Salonika in early 1916, shows a sniper section, the soldier in front holding his Enfield Mk III equipped with an offset scope (either an Aldis or Periscopic Prism) fitted into the awkward, offset PPCo mount. (Author)

trench sniping was undertaken at relatively close ranges, normally under 300yd (274m), for the low-powered optics (2.5× or 3×) were insufficiently powerful and the rifles not overly accurate at longer ranges. H.V. Hesketh-Prichard DSC, MC (1876–1922) was a big-game hunter and competition rifle shooter who through sheer determination managed to persuade the British military high command that sniper training was vital to the British war effort. He recalled:

> I used to have some firing practice at five and six hundred yards [457m and 549m], and when I went to First Army [Sniping] School I gave this up. The chances of hitting a German head at six hundred yards with a telescopic sight, if there is any wind blowing at all, are not great. I came to the conclusion that popping away with telescopic sighted rifles at six hundred yards simply wore out their barrels. We therefore, until warfare became more open, never went back more than four hundred yards [366m].[17]

The Pattern 1913 trials rifle was originally chambered for the advanced high-velocity .276 cartridge, but was never put into production. However, in the guise of the Pattern 1914, it was manufactured in large numbers in the service .303 calibre, and was to see much service in both world wars. (National Firearms Museum, NRAmuseum.com)

There was also the problem of barrel life, Hesketh-Prichard reckoning that 500 rounds would cause sufficient barrel wear to affect accuracy. In addition, the enclosing woodwork also had a detrimental effect. Although the practice was forbidden in the British Army, many Commonwealth snipers cut down the forends of their rifles, providing better accuracy, but the guns themselves needed constant maintenance in order to perform properly. Wet conditions fogged the scopes (waterproofing was yet to be introduced) and the offset design of the scope mount was vulnerable to damage. Private Durst of The King's Royal Rifle Corps spent more than two years as a sniper on the Western Front, and amassed considerable experience in the use and care of his SMLE and scope:

> I used to zero it every time we came out of the line and got new ammunition. I never let anyone touch it … it was quite a good set up but the scope [a PPCo] was a real fiddle to adjust and once it was done I made sure it wasn't mucked about with. I kept it spotless, I was always cleaning the bolt and barrel and some of my chums [in the Sniper section] said I'd wear it away. But I reckoned I only had one chance to get off a shot and I wasn't going to miss.[18]

The long-suffering SMLE was also the hook upon which a number of trench-warfare-inspired inventions were hung. Wire-cutters of several patterns were used, the most common being a 'V' notched bar that screwed to the nosecap in front of the muzzle. Having caught a strand of wire, it then cut the wire by firing a bullet. There was the more complex hinged 'No. 1 Mk I' pattern manufactured in 1916 by Decimals Ltd of Selly Oak

in Birmingham; this genius design relied on using the rifle as a lever, causing two sprung jaws to shut on the offending wire strand. It was very effective due to the leverage imparted by the rifle but alas, whoever thought it up unfortunately missed the vital point that any soldier using it would be doing so standing bolt upright and in full view of the German Army. In addition, he would have a wire belt up to 20ft (6m) deep to deal with. Understandably, most of these devices were jettisoned and they are rare today.

Grenades were a fundamental part of the infantryman's arsenal and any method of lengthening their range was highly useful. Initially a simple rod was screwed to the base of a No. 23 Mills grenade, and fired from an SMLE by means of a blank cartridge. This practice soon ruined the barrel, so rifles were put to one side for grenade use only and their breeches often reinforced with tightly wound copper or steel wire. Later, an improved Mills, the No. 36 Mk I grenade, was introduced, with a circular steel plate screwed to its base. This fitted into a cup discharger and, depending on how the gas vent was adjusted, gave a range of 80–200yd (73–183m). It was very efficient and continued to be used throughout World War II.

Many ideas for useful rifle accessories were tried during the war, one of the least successful being these wire-cutters that clamped to the SMLE's muzzle. They were effective enough, but they required the soldier to stand upright in order to use them. Here Canadian Highlanders at Cambrai, 1917, carry Lee-Enfields with both wire-cutters and grenade cup dischargers. (IWM CO 3305)

Two grenade launchers for the Lee-Enfield. At top, a Mills bomb launcher for a 1915 SMLE, and bottom, a World War II anti-tank grenade launcher for the No. 4. (© Board of Trustees of the Armouries; ex-MoD Pattern Room Collection)

Rifle grenades saw increasing use during the war, and here a soldier poses with an SMLE Mk I mounted in a launching cradle with a Hales rifle grenade in the muzzle. Firing rodded grenades such as this soon ruined the bore. (Author)

WORLD WAR II AND BEYOND

During the inter-war years there was a general consensus throughout the armed forces that the SMLE had served them well through World War I. Its short barrel had not proved a hindrance, particularly where average shooting distances were relatively close, and there was no doubt that its compact dimensions made it ideal for all branches of the services. Even Germany had abandoned the concept of a long infantry rifle, introducing the Kar 98AZ carbine late in the war. But the Enfield was still very expensive to manufacture, with a large number of components requiring a massive input of man-hours. The Pattern 1907 bayonet blade was also regarded as unnecessarily long at 17in (432mm).

Consequently, an improved model, the 'Rifle No. 1 Mk V', was made for troop trials. Between 1922 and 1924 some 20,000 were issued. It was a hybrid of SMLE parts, with an improved aperture rearsight mounted on the receiver above the bolt, and other minor modifications. It was further modified in 1926, when a Mk VI rifle was introduced, although this was manufactured in small numbers. In practical terms, the barrel wall had been thickened and the barrel was now free-floating: it was not attached to the enclosing woodwork, and therefore was unaffected by natural expansions or contractions in the wood. A new bolt-release catch was fitted, the receiver modified and strengthened, and the distinctive one-piece nose-cap was abandoned, the muzzle of the barrel projecting about 2in beyond the forend, although it remained the same overall length as the SMLE. There was a lug system on the muzzle for a short-bladed (7.7in/196mm) 'spike' bayonet to be fitted. An improved aperture rearsight was fitted with a battlesight zeroed for up to 200yd (183m), and graduations for up to 1,300yd (1,189m) in 50yd (46m) increments on the sight body, and the foresight was modified. Although three rifle patterns were made, A, B, and C, only the B was ever used for troop trials. The forend was chequered to improve grip (this was omitted on production rifles) and overall its sleeker lines gave it a more modern look. SAC commented that:

> Generally the new rifle was well-received. The rifle has performed well in trials … with accuracy being much improved over the previous model [the SMLE] and it has been found that target acquisition has been much enhanced due to the improved sighting arrangement … the action is stronger and removal of the bolt has been facilitated by the adoption of the release catch.[19]

With minor improvements it was approved for service on 15 November 1939, as the Rifle No. 4 Mk I, as it turned out, just in the nick of time. Approximately 4,244,700 Enfield No. 4 rifles were manufactured during the war, but Enfield itself produced no more than 460,000 of these.

After World War I the performance of the Lee-Enfield was re-examined and new models, the Mk V and No. 1 Mk VI, were produced. This Mk VI, an early trials model, shows the flip-up aperture rearsight mounted behind the charger bridge, and the distinctive chequering on the stock. (Bob Maze)

THE LEE-ENFIELD EXPOSED

Lee-Enfield No. 4 Mk I

1	Buttplate, incorporating butt-trap access plate	**17**	Magazine
2	Butt-trap, containing barrel pull-through (also oil bottle, not visible)	**18**	Magazine platform
		19	Magazine spring
3	Rear sling swivel	**20**	Sear spring
4	Stock (butt)	**21**	Magazine catch
5	Stock bolt	**22**	Sear
6	Rear hand-guard retaining ring	**23**	Trigger
7	Hand-guard, rear	**24**	Bolt handle
8	Lower band	**25**	Butt socket
9	Lower sling swivel	**26**	Cocking piece
10	Hand-guard, front	**27**	Battlesight Mk II, 300yd and 600yd
11	Forend woodwork	**28**	Leaf pattern rearsight
12	Barrel, exposing rifling	**29**	Bolt head catch
13	Upper band	**30**	Charger guide
14	Foresight protector and foresight	**31**	Bolt body
15	Muzzle	**32**	Bolt head
16	Chamber		

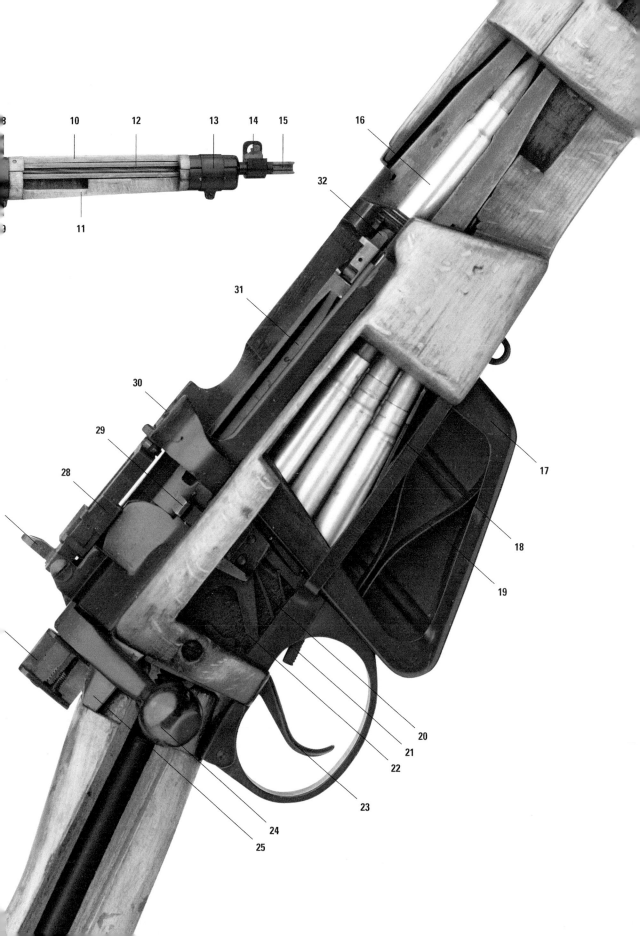

Far more were made by contractors based at Fazakerly, near Liverpool; Shirley, in Birmingham; Maltby, near Sheffield; Long Branch in Canada; and Savage Arms in Massachusetts, who between them produced approximately 1,236,000. The reason for this was simply that with war looming, production at RSAF Enfield had already been largely allocated to the manufacture of machine guns and revolvers, and Small Heath at Birmingham was concentrating on machine guns and anti-tank rifles. (By 1943, however, the .55in Boys anti-tank rifle had been rendered obsolete by improvements in tank armour, and production ceased.) In 1943 a Mk IV cost £7 15s to produce (£258 at today's values) if home-produced timber was used for stocking.

Early wartime production of the new rifle simply couldn't keep pace with demand, although the situation wasn't helped by air raids in late 1940 that badly disrupted production in Birmingham. Despite the weapon having being approved on 15 November 1939, almost no No. 4 rifles reached the armed forces until the latter half of 1942. That the basic design was sound is evidenced by the fact that only one officially revised model was introduced during the war years, the No. 4 Mk I*,

A whole generation of small arms in use near a Japanese strongpoint in Burma. The second soldier (counting foreground-to-background) has a venerable SMLE, the next a Bren gun, the third and fourth Enfield No. 4s; the fifth crouching man holds one of the many Sten variants. (IWM SE 3757)

approved on 14 June 1941; even then, changes were minimal, the most significant being the adoption of a two-groove barrel, although both five- and six-groove versions were still produced. It remained Britain's front-line service rifle in conjunction with huge numbers of re-issued No. 1 Mk III rifles, which were used widely in operational theatres outside of Europe.

One of the greatest headaches regarding production of the No. 4 was caused by a lack of proper quality control, which led to problems with the barrels, rearsights, bolts and contract-manufactured magazines. On many rifles the bolts jammed, as they had been machined slightly oversize, and magazine feed-plates could stick due to weak springs. Some contract magazines could not accept ten rounds of ammunition. Occasionally rifles were issued that suffered from all of these problems, to the utter despair of unit armourers. The bores on many rifles were very poorly machined and tolerances were widely variable '... when passing the bores for gauging – anything from .301 to .305 inch was passed as fit for use. Some of the rifles were terrible.'[20] Worse still was the quality of the steel used in some barrels:

> I remember in late 1942 I was in charge of a party firing on a 30 yard [28m] range using No. 4 rifles. One of the men had fired three shots and scored three bulls on the miniature target; I noticed that he was taking a long time to get his fourth shot away and asked the reason. He said that he could not see his foresight. He was quite right, the barrel had bent so much![21]

But there was probably more criticism over the sighting arrangements on the early No. 4s than anything else. The two-position aperture sight was confusing to use and the poor fit of the rearsight itself made accurate shooting nearly impossible. After a couple of largely worthless modifications, a new pattern of micro-adjustable rearsight with single 200yd (183m) battlesight was introduced, which finally solved the problem. There were only two other major patterns of the No. 4 rifle manufactured, one in response to demands for a more compact weapon for jungle fighting, and this was the Rifle No. 5 Mk I, generally but unofficially known as the 'jungle carbine'. The other was the sniping variant, the No. 4 Mk I (T).

RIFLE, No. 5 Mk I – THE JUNGLE CARBINE

Initially conceived as a trials piece, this lightened No. 4 underwent testing and was adopted officially on 12 September 1944, although it had already been in production for some months by then. Basically a No. 4 with a 20.5in (521mm) barrel, it was some 5in (127mm) shorter than the ordinary rifle. As a result its range and accuracy were seriously compromised, although the sights were still graduated to 800yd (732m), and a large flash-hider was fitted that required the use of a new pattern of

The rearsight of a No. 4 Mk I, made by Savage Arms in the United States. It was a great improvement over earlier patterns and provided a sharper sight picture for the shooter. (National Firearms Museum, NRAmuseum.com)

knife bayonet. A thick rubber recoil-pad was appended to the butt, but this did little to reduce the tooth-jarring recoil, and unsurprisingly it proved unpopular with soldiers, despite being light and very useful for close-quarter fighting. Aside from jungle issue, they were also used by troops of 6th Airborne Division when they occupied Denmark in 1945. Production ceased at the end of 1947.

The No. 5 'jungle carbine' with No. 5 Mk I knife bayonet. (National Firearms Museum, NRAmuseum.com)

THE No. 4 (T) SNIPING RIFLE

At the outbreak of World War II there were about 2,000 Pattern 1914 Mk I* W (T) sniping rifles in store, mostly with Aldis or PPCo scopes mated to a German-inspired claw mount. It was an excellent combination, but the rifles were no longer in production and neither were the telescopes, so while some additional rifles were assembled from stored weapons and scopes by Alex Martin of Glasgow, an alternative needed to be quickly sourced. That some new form of optical sight and sniping rifle was needed was unquestionable, and fortunately a suitable telescope was not difficult to find. A sturdy 3× scope, designated the No. 32 Mk I, had been designed for use with the Bren gun, but never put into wartime production in its intended role. Some early-production examples of the scope were successfully tested in May 1940 mated to the only conceivable rifle that could be used, the No. 4.

Thus in mid-1940, 1,400 early trials rifles (manufactured between 1929 and 1933) were selected and converted for sniping use. (The author's own No. 4 is one such, manufactured in 1931 and fitted with the earliest-known production No. 32 scope.) The conversion involved a considerable amount of modification, two steel pads being fitted on the left of the receiver to which the cast-iron scope mounting bracket was screwed. The rifles were re-stocked and bedded, and a cheek-pad was fitted to the butt.

Initial impressions during trials were very favourable. The scopes were ranged from 100yd to 1,000yd (91–914m), with elevation and windage drums that had click adjustment in increments of 2 minutes of angle (MOA – an MOA equates to 1in at 100yd, 2in at 200yd, and so forth). Although the scope and mount were heavy at 2lb 8oz (1.2kg) they were very robust, one sniper dryly remarking that if the Germans got too close he could club them to death with his scope. Accuracy was good too, the rifles proving better at longer ranges than shorter, due in part to barrel harmonics and bullet design, and ranges well in excess of 600yd (549m) were quite feasible given suitable conditions.

It was soon decided that the time-consuming process of factory-modifying each rifle was unsustainable due to the needs of wartime production, so in late September 1942 Holland & Holland of London undertook the conversion of all of Britain's No. 4 sniping rifles, at a unit cost of £2 7s 6d per rifle (£280 today). Added to the initial manufacturing cost of the rifles, this made them quite expensive, but there was little alternative, as British and Commonwealth soldiers were facing a well-equipped enemy with plentiful supplies of sniping rifles. The rifles selected were virtually all from BSA Shirley production (although some converted Long Branch rifles have also surfaced) and all were weapons that had proven to be particularly accurate when test-fired. A scope was individually allocated to each rifle and serial-number-matched. They were not directly interchangeable, for any replacement scope would need to be re-zeroed, and possibly have the mount slightly modified to suit. One ex-armourer mentioned to the author that a wooden mallet was often the preferred method.

There were, inevitably, some modifications to the telescopes, and the No. 32 went through three patterns: Mk I, Mk I/II, and Mk III (although the Mk III wasn't officially accepted into service until October 1944).

Snipers training with Lee-Enfield No. 4 (T) rifles. These weapons were individually rebuilt to very high standards by Holland & Holland of London, and proved to be both accurate and reliable; many are still in use today. (Clive Law)

Improvements included: removing the sliding brass sunshade from the ocular end of the scope (on recoil it often cut open the firer's eyebrow); strengthening the internal springs to cure a weakness with the drum adjustment; improved lens assembly; waterproofing the bodies; providing finer 1-MOA drum adjustment; and, eventually, blooming the lenses to improve light-gathering. The rifles had modified rearsights fitted, with the battlesight removed to facilitate bolt removal; mounting pads were staked to the screws to prevent them undoing, and an American Pattern 1908 sniper sling was provided that attached to a specially fitted sling-swivel just forward of the magazine. The No. 4 (T) proved to be an excellent sniping rifle, and was used in every theatre of war. In total some 24,442 were manufactured.

The cessation of hostilities in 1945 did not mark the end of the line for the venerable Lee-Enfield, though, for the No. 4 rifle continued to see service into the 1950s. However, the insistence of the USA that a new NATO standard cartridge, the 7.62mm (.308in), be adopted in 1953 was the death-knell for the old bolt-action model. Although several hundred were converted as the 'Rifle, Series L8' by fitting 7.62mm barrels and modified magazines (models designated A1 to A5 were produced), the results were inconclusive, the relative benefits of conversion being outweighed by the cost of modifying what was a basically obsolete design. In addition, they were time-consuming to convert and most other NATO countries had by then moved to semi-automatic rifles. Britain had been toying with introducing its own design, the advanced .280in EM-2, but due to political manoeuvrings by the USA on the eve of doing so, it was forced to drop it in 1954 in favour of a new semi-automatic rifle, the 7.62mm FN/FAL. However, a variant of the No. 4 (T) was to remain in service as Britain's front-line sniping weapon until August 1970, as during testing the L8 had proven to be unexpectedly accurate; from this arose the L42A1 sniping rifle, chambered for the NATO 7.62mm cartridge. The L42A1 was half-stocked, with a heavy, free-floating barrel and a No. 32 Mk III scope graduated in metres, but it was, to all intents, an upgraded No. 4 (T). It remained a very capable rifle, though, and was to see service with the UK armed forces until 1982.

USE
Bolt-action soldiering

CRITICS AND COMBAT

Historically, few new arms introduced into service have ever arrived perfectly functional. Even today, with the almost limitless ability of computers to design and undertake sophisticated manufacturing processes, there have been several problematical small arms adopted. The US M16, Austrian Steyr AUG and Britain's own SA80 all suffered from teething troubles to a greater or lesser extent, and the Enfields were no exception. At the outset, the new rifles received harsh criticism when first introduced into service:

> In the matter of the Magazine Rifle, which is now the subject of discussion and experiment, the War Office has not told the truth to the English people. On the contrary, it has done its best to conceal the truth, to baffle independent inquiry, and to stifle criticism. The proceedings have been shrouded in perhaps a denser cloud than usual of official reticence and mystery. But the official report from the School of Musketry at Hythe ... has been suppressed because it contains severe and damaging criticism.[22]

Shortcomings with the new rifle had caused a furore not only within the ranks of the military, but also among target shooters in the National Rifle Association (NRA), who believed that the new arm was a retrograde step. Today, it is hard to comprehend just what passions this debate aroused in the normally passive British breast, but at the turn of the century, target shooting was a national sport to the extent that matches were given several column inches in *The Times* every week, as were the weather forecasts for forthcoming meetings. It was, in short, taken very seriously indeed. The first letters berating the Army Council for meddling with an apparently already efficient service rifle appeared in 1898, and much doubt was expressed about the safety of the new bolt-action rifles:

> We are fully aware that it is not the function of the bolt-head screw to take the shock of explosion … what we mean to affirm is that [it] does suffer severely from the jar of explosion and gives way under a fatally large number of cases. What is the precise degree of efficiency and trustworthiness of a soldier's – not as an experimentalist's – weapon?[23]

Inevitably, over time there arose a gradual acceptance that the bolt action was actually an improvement over the Martini. However, the modifications proposed that resulted in the Mk I* and Mk II versions were still not good enough for the pundits:

Canadian soldiers carefully inching their way up a kopjie during the Second Boer War. They are holding Lee-Metfords with Model 1888 bayonets attached. (© Hulton-Deutsch Collection/Corbis)

We are now told that ... the rifle in its present form has serious defects ... but we are asked to believe that the Mk. 2 will be perfection. If the Lee-Speed rifle [Lee-Metford Mk I] is so splendid a weapon as to justify the costly revolution in the arming of our troops ... why are experiments carefully limited ... and the reports of them carefully edited ... Why are the most authoritative judgements suppressed?[24]

Admittedly, the new magazine rifles cost more than twice as much as the old Martini-Henry, but they were far more complex to manufacture and infinitely more sophisticated. Finding out exactly what the soldier in the field thought of the early issue of these guns is difficult today, for most field trials were reported on by armourers, officers and expert riflemen and the results written up by SAC staff. Generally the soldiers themselves left behind little in the way of comments on their new weapons. There are just a few surviving accounts of the use of Lee-Metfords on the North-West Frontier, in the Sudan and during the Second Boer War. (Although the Lee-Enfield had been introduced in late 1895, British troops on colonial service were often to be found still using the earlier models.) During the battle of Omdurman, at Atbara (2 September 1898), the power of the new magazine rifle was unleashed for all to see:

The Mahdists approached, continually gaining ground to the left, and stretching out towards Kerreri. Then a forest of white banners appeared over the shoulder of Surgham ridge, and about the same time the guns began to fire on both sides. For a little while the infantry watched the shells exploding in the air in front of the attack. Battalion by battalion, the Guards first at 2,700 yards [2,469m], then the Seaforths at 2,000 yards [1,829m], and the others following according to the taste and fancy of their commanding officers, the British division began to fire. As the range shortened Maxwell's Sudanese brigade, and a moment later MacDonald's, joined in the fusillade, until by 6.45 more than 12,000 infantry were engaged in that mechanical scattering of death which the polite nations of the earth have brought to such monstrous perfection. They fired steadily and stolidly, without hurry or excitement, for the enemy were far away and the officers careful. Besides, the soldiers were interested in the work and took great pains. But presently the mere physical act became tedious. The tiny figures seen over the slide of the back-sight seemed a little larger, but also fewer at each successive volley. The rifles grew hot – so hot that they had to be changed for those of the reserve companies. The empty cartridge-cases, tinkling to the ground, formed small but growing heaps beside each man. And all the time out on the plain on the other side bullets were shearing through flesh, smashing and splintering bone; blood spouted from terrible wounds; valiant men were struggling on through a hell of whistling metal, exploding shells, and spurting dust, suffering, despairing, dying. Such was the first phase of the battle of Omdurman.[25]

Meanwhile, the Mahdists launched a frontal attack:

> The debris of the 'White Flags' joined the centre, and the whole 14,000 pressed forward against the *zeriba*, gradually spreading out and abandoning their dense formations, and gradually slowing down. At about 800 yards [732m] from the British division the advance ceased, and they could make no headway. Opposite, the Sudanese who were armed only with the Martini-Henry rifle ... came within 300 yards [274m]; and one brave old man, carrying a flag, fell at 150 paces [about 130m] from the shelter trench. As soon as the leading company commanded by Captain Maxwell [of The Lincolnshire Regiment] cleared the right of MacDonald's brigade, they formed line, and opened an independent fire obliquely across the front of the Sudanese. Groups of Dervishes in twos and threes were then within a hundred yards [91m]. The great masses were within 300 yards [274m]. The independent firing lasted two minutes, during which the whole regiment deployed. Its effect was to clear away the leading groups of Arabs. The deployment having been accomplished with the loss of a dozen men, including Colonel Sloggett, who fell shot through the breast while attending to the wounded, section volleys were ordered. With excellent discipline the independent firing was instantly stopped, and the battalion began with machine-like regularity to carry out the principles of modern musketry, for which their training had efficiently prepared them and their rifles were admirably suited. They fired on an average sixty rounds per man, and finally repulsed the attack.[26]

The result of the fight was a catastrophic defeat for the Arabs: subsequent estimates gave their losses at 9,700 killed and 13,000 wounded for the loss of 48 British killed and 340 wounded. Despite the verbal battering the new magazine rifle had received in the press, particularly in respect of its poor accuracy at long range and predilection for jamming when hot, there was little evidence that it underperformed during the battle. The fact that fire was opened on the Mahdists at ranges of 2,700yd (2,469m) was in itself quite extraordinary and such a feat would have been utterly impossible with the Martini.

In the face of this apparent success, many die-hard sports shooters began to look at the new rifles with a more open mind, and commercial sales improved rapidly as a consequence. Ever busy policing the colonies, the Army had little time to wait before a new threat developed in Africa when Boer settlers, always dismissive of British interests, had from the 1830s begun openly to challenge imperial authority. This time, however, things were different, for by the 1880s the Boers were extremely well armed themselves with the latest magazine rifles and most could outshoot the average British soldier. One of the major problems facing the British troops was the distances involved. At this time British soldiers were not taught to estimate extreme ranges, but were ordered by NCOs or officers at what distances to fire; in the vastness of the veldt, virtually no one could calculate this with any accuracy:

We came under fire from the Boers … from a point so distant we could not see them. Our cavalrymen dismounted and pulled their carbines from their scabbards, but were powerless to reply, not being able to determine from whence came the fusillade. Men began to drop, and the horses took fright as one after another was hit, the colonel ordering them to safety behind some low hills. The men lay down … shortly the first infantry arrived but despite the use of binoculars by their officers, the whereabouts of the troublesome Boers still remained a mystery.[27]

The short-range cavalry carbines proved largely useless and many mounted troopers carried Long Lees: 'One cavalryman dismounted and took steady aim with a long rifle, killing three Boers with as many shots, before mounting his horse and galloping forwards.'[28] The display of such skill was a rare event, though, for generally the Boer riflemen were able to target and shoot British soldiers from extreme range; this was horribly evidenced during the battle of Spion Kop (23–24 January 1900), when it was conclusively shown that weapons technology did not necessarily overcome skill-at-arms.

A Boer kommando, holding a mix of Mauser M1895 and Lee-Metford rifles. These were the best rifles then available and the Boers were expert in their use. (Author)

The Boers had not taken the trouble to entrench themselves on the top of the spur, that they had in other places, probably because an attack from the quarter from which we delivered it was deemed improbable; but the great rocks made the position one of enormous natural strength. On the flanks on the other surrounding features they were strongly entrenched. This portion of the position we discovered afterwards to be under Schalk Burgher's command. On arrival at the top of the hill we found that a few Boers had retired down the further slopes and were making terribly good practice against any of our riflemen who showed theirs heads over the sky line. It was then that Colonel Riddell, who all through the attack had worked wonders by his example, stood up to try and discover where these sharpshooters were located, with the result which has been so much deplored by all who knew him [he was shot dead].[29]

British casualties at Spion Kop amounted to 1,500 dead and wounded – 235 were killed on the hilltop alone – while Boer casualties numbered 335 dead and wounded, mostly due to artillery fire. To a certain extent the blame lay not with the soldiers, but the new rifles, for there had been earlier complaints that while the rifles were adequate for volley fire, for accurate shooting the sights were poor. These complaints were largely dismissed at the time, but subsequent tests on new rifles showed that many were leaving the factories incorrectly graduated, to the extent that some Sparkbrook-produced weapons were zeroing 20in (508mm) to the right at 200yd (183m). Many others showed similar errors, while all were so badly undersighted that they were shooting between 50 and 70yd (46–64m) short at 600yd (549m). This performance was clearly hopeless for achieving any sort of accuracy, particularly at the combat distances involved in South Africa, and all rifles destined for service there were hurriedly modified with improved rearsight leaves and an adjustable foresight. However, not all of the rifles were so badly affected, besides which during much of the fighting distances were often so close that shooting was almost point-blank, and the Boers suffered accordingly from British rifle fire.

> During my absence about fifty [British] soldiers had run forward to surrender, but otherwise things were going none too well. We were sustaining heavy casualties from the English 'schans' immediately in front of us, and the men grew restive under the galling point-blank fire, a thing not to be wondered at, for the moral effect of Lee-Metford volleys at twenty yards [18m] must be experienced to be appreciated. The English troops lay so near that one could have tossed a biscuit among them, and whilst the losses which they were causing us were only too evident, we on our side did not know that we were inflicting even greater damage upon them. Our own casualties lay hideously among us, but theirs were screened from view behind the breastwork, so that the comfort of knowing that we were giving worse than we received was denied us. The sun became hotter and hotter, and we had neither food nor water. Around us lay scores of dead and wounded men, a depressing sight, and ... as the hours dragged on a trickle of men slipped down the hill, and in spite of his watchful eye this gradual wastage so depleted our strength that long before nightfall we were holding the blood-spattered ledge with a mere handful of rifles. I wanted to go too, but the thought of Isaac and my other friends saved me from deserting ... the heavy close-range rifle-fire continued hour after hour, and the tale of losses mounted while we lay in the blazing heat. I saw a strange incident during the morning. Near me was a German named von Brusewitz. He had been an officer in the German army, but ... he seemed bent on getting killed, for although we warned him not to expose himself too recklessly, he paid no heed. As the English soldiers were so close to us this was sheer folly, and after he had tempted providence several times the inevitable happened. I saw him rise once more, and, lighting a cigarette, puff away careless of the flying bullets until we heard a thud, and he fell dead within a few feet of me, shot through the head.[30]

Inevitably, when the war ended there was an investigation by SAC into the performance of the rifles. Criticism over their accuracy notwithstanding, the new rifles appeared to have acquitted themselves quite well. The sighting deficiencies had to be properly addressed of course, as did some

problems with the magazine and bolt design, but overall it was considered that the guns themselves were robust and easy to maintain in the field, albeit somewhat overly long and heavy. One other significant problem to be solved concerned the slowness of loading, for Boer Mausers were clip-loaded and much faster to recharge. Experimentation with the new short rifle was already under way, though, and the decision to adopt it wholesale for all branches of the armed services was without doubt a brave one, and unusually forward-thinking for SAC, who were not generally regarded as radical.

If the adoption of the bolt-action rifle had caused outrage in the press, the furore caused over the decision to issue a single short pattern of rifle was even greater and things became decidedly more heated with the adoption of the SMLE Mk I. A small book could be devoted to the correspondence, but the argument against was basically straightforward – the new rifle, with a barrel 5in (127mm) shorter, simply could not be as accurate as the longer-barrelled rifles and would prove totally disastrous in combat:

> Science and universal experience are at one in assuring us that … a long barrel will always shoot better than a short one. It is hardly possible to make it [a short barrel] better for work in war, unless the long barrel is very bad indeed. It must have occurred to other nations that a short barrel would be more handy and lighter than a long one, but they have all declined to carry the sacrifice of ballistic efficiency … any further than it is carried in our existing [long] rifles. Has the short rifle any special merits not possessed by the long rifle? All that can be said for it is that it is 'handier' – a vague word – by reason of its shortness. The manufacture of the new rifle ought to be stopped … there are other objections to a short rifle which ought to be fatal to it. These are the loss of reach of the bayonet, which must be a heavy handicap to the soldier, who as a rule, shoots badly.[31]

The turn-of-the-century criticism of the SMLE's shortness was proved unfounded in World War I, when the compact rifle proved admirably suited to use in the trenches. However, when equipped with its bayonet the SMLE was too long for close-quarters fighting, and trench raiders preferred to use it without. This photo is entitled 'A Canadian Trench Raid', but the fact that the men have canvas breech covers in place, and are wearing cumbersome greatcoats, raises doubts about what is really happening. (IWM CO 876)

Many of the writers of these letters and tracts were serving soldiers as well as Bisley shooters, and their entrenched opinions underlined the widening gulf between the requirements of the Army and the sports shooter. The anonymous writer of this letter neatly summed up the dichotomy facing SAC, namely that while a short rifle was lighter and easier to handle, this convenience was countered by some loss of accuracy. The crucial point here was that by the first decade of the 20th century the traditional requirements of target shooters had become increasingly at variance with those of modern combat soldiers. Shooting at known distances at a fixed target was very different from facing a charging enemy. Besides, British soldiers who were taught to shoot upon command would rarely need to utilize the long-range performance of their rifles, a salient fact ignored by most sports shooters. There was also the tendency (and it is common even today) for armies to set the standard of their weapons and training by the experiences gained in the most recent conflict in which they had fought, without considering that any new war may be of a totally different nature. The Second Boer War was not going to happen again, but a European war was highly likely. Unofficial accuracy tests were even carried out at Bisley by some of these pen-wielding riflemen. The results were widely reported in the press, apparently indicating that the new rifle was deficient in almost every respect:

> The short rifle is badly balanced ... the sights are not adapted for snap firing ... the recoil was considerably heavier ... the accuracy is diminished ... all noticed a great flash of flame from the short barrel ... as a weapon for cavalry, the short rifle is an advance on the carbine. These gentlemen ... are unanimous in condemning the reduction in length of barrel, not only because the barrel is rendered less accurate but also because ... they found it unhandy and ill-balanced.[32]

Ironically, of the testers, several, including Major Richardson, Captain Varley and Private (later Lieutenant) George Grey, went on to become sniper instructors, while armourer Sergeant Fulton was a successful sniper, all using the same short rifle that they had decried a decade earlier.

The subsequent re-organization of the Territorial Army in the Haldane Reforms of 1907 was long overdue, and was the result of much debate not only about its future role in war but the poor level of training it received, in particular the lack of suitable musketry drill.[33] Assurances were given that all soldiers, Regular and Territorial, would be trained to a far higher level of competency, and a revised *Musketry Training Manual, Part 1* was introduced in 1909.

Teaching soldiers to use their initiative was something that did not sit easily with the Regular Army; soldiers were, after all, there to carry things and obey orders, but the Territorial Army contained some well-educated and intelligent men and the Army was forced to recognize the fact. At last, soldiers were taught how to estimate ranges, understand basic ballistics, fire at moving targets and allow for deflection. Above all, they learned to handle and fire their weapons with a very high degree of proficiency. It

By 1909 musketry training was being taken seriously. Here soldiers of the Regular Army train at what appears to be a reasonably long distance, possibly 500yd (461m) or more. (Peter Smith)

was expected that most line infantrymen could aim and fire at a rate of 15rpm, but many could easily exceed that figure. Private Frank Richards of The Royal Welsh Fusiliers recalled that 'The three of us had been marksmen all through our soldiering; each of us could get off twenty-five aimed rounds a minute.'[34] With the outbreak of war in August 1914, the men of the pitifully small British Regular Army (247,000 strong in 1914, of whom about 125,000 comprised the BEF) and their SMLEs were given their first real chance to demonstrate their capabilities. As German forces swept across Western Europe in the 'race to the sea', the BEF fought a series of pitched battles against overwhelming odds. In the wake of what had been inflicted on the Army during the South African campaign, there existed a far greater awareness of the importance of good shooting, and the first contacts made with German forces showed that the BEF could take on the enemy with consistently better results than before.

Private Richards, cited above, faced the Germans during the First Battle of Ypres (19 October–22 November 1914): 'We were advancing by platoons in extended order over open country, when rifle-fire opened out from somewhere in front. We judged it to come from a fair sized wood about 600 yards [549m] away, and laying down opened out with rapid fire at it.'[35] Permitting regular soldiers to assess ranges and open fire of their own volition would have been unthinkable a decade before, but here it paid dividends. Shortly afterwards the Germans began to clear a firepath in front of Richards' trench, fatally underestimating the skill of the riflemen in front of them:

Methods of launching grenades improved greatly during World War I. Here, Indian infantry use an attachment to fire the No. 23 grenade. The short rod on the grenade didn't damage the bore as severely as earlier models, but would nevertheless have drastically shortened the barrel life. (Author)

49

We had our rifles resting on the bank … and it was impossible to miss at that distance. We had downed half-a-dozen men before they realised what was happening; then they commenced to jump back into the trench … but we bowled them over like rabbits. It put me in mind of firing at the 'running man' on a peace-time course of musketry. We had expended our magazines, which held ten rounds – there wasn't a live enemy to be seen and the whole affair had lasted half a minute. We quickly reloaded … turned around and ran towards our trench. Miles and I did not know what narrow squeaks we had until someone noticed a bullet-hole through Miles's trousers and two more through my sleeve.[36]

TRENCH WARFARE

If nothing else, the German soldiers taking part in those early battles rapidly learned to have a very healthy respect for the speed and accuracy of British rifle fire, and the First Battle of Ypres became known as *Der Kindermond bei Ypern* or 'The massacre of the Innocents', in memory of the 25,000 young German student volunteers who died there under the muzzles of the BEF's rifles. The ten-round capacity of the Lee-Enfield was also an advantage when on the defensive, enabling a fearsome level of sustained fire to be maintained. In fact, so deadly was the volume of rifle fire that one German commander is reported as saying that the British units that were attacked were all armed with machine guns. This was quite untrue, of course. In fact the British Army was extremely short of machine guns – at the time a British infantry battalion had two guns (until 1915, then four; German battalions in 1914 had six).

The gritty reality of trench warfare soon became familiar to British and Commonwealth soldiers. In a trench on Gallipoli, an Australian sniper holds his Mk III, waiting for the signal from his observer to make a snap-shot. Oddly, he has his bayonet fitted, which would not have aided accurate shooting. (Australian War Memorial)

Nevertheless, the comment was a matter of considerable pride to the British soldiers.

Although the German attacks of 1914 were temporarily halted, the war still had a long way to go, and the price paid by the BEF was heavy, for it lost more than 58,000 men and with them the skills of the Regular Army and its superb marksmanship. From 1915 the war was to go underground, opening a new phase in the life of the Lee-Enfield. Although the SMLE had clearly not been designed with trench warfare in mind, it proved to be admirably suited to it. Its compact size, close-fitting curved bolt handle and blunt muzzle could have been custom-made for the confined trenches, unlike the German Mauser Gew 98, whose long bolt handle sat awkwardly at right angles to the receiver. Moreover, its excessive length and projecting muzzle snagged continually on clothing, equipment and wire, making it clumsy for trench use.

One problem that had continually been referred to by the pre-war pundits was the unsuitability of the Enfield for snap-shooting, as they believed that the rearsight was too far from the firer's eye. In practice, however, once they became familiar with the rifle, men adapted quickly to its quirks. The finest exponents of this risky form of shooting were undoubtedly the Australians, New Zealanders and Canadians, particularly indigenous Canadians, whose incredibly sharp eyes and reflexes made them some of the most feared riflemen on the Western Front. Despite the criticisms, the SMLE actually proved more than adequate for the task, its sighting arrangement posing no problem at all for making fast shots and its short length making rapid target acquisition easier. Many excelled with it. Private Henry Norwest, MM and Bar, aka Henry Louis North-West-Wind, was one example. A Metis (French/Cree) Indian, he was noted for the speed with which he could aim and shoot, raising his rifle, aiming and firing all in one smooth motion, then being able to reload and fire again in under two seconds. Norwest's official total of kills was in excess of 115. He was shot and killed by a German sniper on 18 August 1918 and is buried in Warvillers Cemetery Extension, France.

Snap-shooting wasn't perhaps the ideal method for dealing with the enemy, though, for as Captain H.V. Hesketh-Prichard commented: 'men who tried snap-shooting over the parapet seldom lived very long, the Germans being plentifully equipped with telescopic rifles'.[37] Most men were not so blessed with the required abilities, and as the war progressed many conscripts arrived at the front with barely any idea how to even shoot their rifles. When 18-year-old Fred Mowbray arrived in France in 1918 he so terrified his instructor with his utter lack of rifle-shooting ability that he was made company Lewis gunner, his sergeant considering it less likely he would miss with a machine gun.[38] He commented many years later that he had fired only ten live rounds during his training.

During the battle for Amiens in 1918, Gordon Highlanders watch over the open plains above the city. The open landscape meant that shooting at ranges of 600yd (545m) and beyond was commonplace and required a level of skill that mostly no longer existed, as few late-war soldiers had the shooting ability of the men of the old BEF. (IWM Q 10785)

Off duty, the cleaning of rifles was regarded as being of paramount importance. Here, British soldiers clean their Lee-Enfields under the watchful gaze of an NCO. The man at centre appears to be dropping a pull-through into the barrel. (IWM Q 32894)

As the war progressed, the practicalities and limitations of the SMLE became more evident. It was without doubt a fine general combat rifle, although its close manufacturing tolerances made it intolerant of mud, which abounded on the Western Front. One solution was the introduction of a canvas breech cover that clipped over the bolt and receiver and kept the worst of the dirt out. Preventing the muzzle from blocking up was a serious problem, for dirt inside the barrel could cause it to bulge or even burst on firing, and men devised many methods of trying to prevent this. The practice of pushing a small piece of cork from a beer or wine bottle into the muzzle was popular. In theory this would be blown out by the pressure wave in front of the bullet, but it wasn't the safest of methods. An old sock slid over the nose cap was popular and infinitely safer, but constant cleaning was really the only way of ensuring reliable functioning.

Although a pull-through bore cleaner and oil bottle were housed in the butt-trap, finding cleaning cloth and sufficient lubricant was always a problem when in the line. 'When I could I used bits of shirt-tail to clean the barrel and once, when we were exchanging our filthy clothes for clean ones

The Aisne, 1914 (previous pages)

Rifle Brigade regulars of 11th Infantry Brigade, BEF, open fire at extreme range on advancing German infantry. They are armed with a mix of charger-loading Lee-Enfield Mk I and Short, Magazine Lee-Enfield Mk I rifles. The soldiers of the BEF were proud of their rapid-fire ability; 15 aimed rounds per minute was easily achievable, but experienced riflemen could manage 25 shots per minute. Firing at such a rate caused the breech and bolt in the Enfield to overheat and jam, so in order to continue firing soldiers had to find rifles dropped by fallen comrades. So intense was the British rifle fire that General Alexander von Kluck believed the British Army was largely armed with machine-guns. By using their dial (volley or long-range) sights, they were able to engage enemy troops at ranges in excess of 1,000yd (914m).

at the bath-house, one of the ASC [Army Service Corps] blokes looked at my ragged shirt and said "Blimey chum, you'd better have another bath, you've got rats living in your trousers."[39] Even so, a dirty barrel or rusty bolt was justifiably regarded as a serious offence, and would get a man put on a charge for failing to keep his rifle clean. Overall, though, the Mk III acquitted itself very well, and to the very bitter end of the fighting British and Commonwealth soldiers believed they had the finest battle rifle of any country. Inevitably, though, after the cessation of hostilities, there were some questions about its performance that needed answering.

THE POST-WAR ENFIELD

Long-range accuracy had never been a strong point of the SMLE and this was exacerbated by the practice of totally enclosing the barrel with wood, for in wet conditions the wood swelled and put pressure on the barrel. In addition, there was an internally mounted spring underneath the fore-part of the barrel that placed pressure on it in an attempt to maintain its rigidity. In fact it probably had the opposite effect. One rifle instructor, Major B. Penberthy, calculated that moving a barrel merely one-hundredth of an inch out of true would result in the point of impact being 9in off-centre at 100yd (229mm at 91m).[40] It is surprising that such all-encompassing furniture was adopted, for sports shooters knew that the most accurate rifles were those that were only half-stocked, with nothing at all touching the barrel beyond the breech, a practice well understood then and continued to this day.

Soldiers wait for approaching troops during the battle for the Lys, 1918. A fixed bayonet radically affected the accuracy of the rifle, and combat soldiers generally preferred not to shoot with them fitted. Despite this, the order 'fix bayonets' was still widely regarded as a morale booster. (IWM Q 6617)

There were other practical considerations, too. A long bayonet was needed to match the reach of the Mauser (which in itself was far too long). The early Pattern 1907 bayonet had a hooked quillon – a curled lower guard meant to trap an opponent's blade. In reality, of course, it trapped everything else as well; as a result, post-1913 issue bayonets were supplied without the quillon. In use, the long blade sometimes snapped, or jammed in the victim's body: 'I ran through a Jerry as he came out of his dugout, but the blade stuck in his ribs and I couldn't get the bloody thing out. He was screaming and pulling at it and all I could do was fire a shot, the recoil jerking it out. Another Jerry appeared and ran to the dead man, crying, "*mein bruder, mein bruder*".'[41] Generally it was agreed that a shorter, stronger blade would be more practical and a new design would enable it to be mass-produced more cheaply and quickly. The designers at Enfield continued to try to find ways of improving the rifle and when war broke out yet again in September 1939, the Army was to be equipped with the No. 4, which was arguably to prove to be the best battle rifle of World War II.

THE LEE-ENFIELD IN WORLD WAR II

While many people think of the SMLE as the archetypal rifle of the Great War and the No. 4 as its successor in World War II, nothing could be further from the truth. Both the No. 1 Mk III and the No. 4 were issued in huge numbers, there being plentiful stocks of the earlier models held in government arsenals. Anyone who has watched film footage of the retreat from Dunkirk in 1940 will see that it is the SMLE that is universally being carried, as supplies of the new weapon had not reached the BEF. Private Bill Smith recalled:

> We hadn't stopped retreating for what seemed like weeks. We'd had almost no sleep and only the food we could scavenge from trucks and sometimes the dead. I'd no kit left apart from a small haversack, my rifle and ammunition. I kept the rifle as spotless as I could, as we didn't know when Jerry might appear, but we never saw a live one. I never actually fired it until we were waiting on the beach. We were a sitting duck for the Stukas, who bombed us without mercy. After they had dropped their bombs, they turned and came down low to strafe us and they were quite slow as they were turning. So the Sergeant Major got us into rifle squads and we let fly with rapid fire as they came over. We'd shoot just ahead of them, to allow for deflection ... one afternoon ... we must have hit the pilot because it jerked upwards then turned on its back and crashed into the sea. Oh, you could have heard the cheers from Dover, it really buoyed us up it did ... we wondered if they were more cautious afterwards because they never came so low again. When we got back to England and were re-equipped we had to hand our old rifles in ... many of the men were very unhappy about being issued with the new one, it was never as good.[42]

He also remembered that the weapon he was issued with was date-stamped 1914, an early wartime production No. 1 Mk III. In fact, a number of these rifles carried during the later desert and jungle campaigns were of pre-World War I manufacture.

When the No. 4 was issued it was not initially a roaring success, particularly with old soldiers, amongst whom word began to circulate that the 'new' rifle was not a patch on the old. To a great extent the problem was caused simply by the difference between the complex patterns of sights used. Matters were not improved, though, by the recommendation of the Small Arms School that test firing be done with and without the bayonet in position, which naturally affected the zero of the rifle. Zeroing a rifle with fixed bayonet was an anathema to any soldier, as Captain Charles Shore, a musketry instructor, noted tersely: 'As a rifleman I detested the business of bayonet fixing and would have none of it.'[43] Thus the first aperture on the battlesight was calibrated for 300yd (274m) with fixed bayonet, but correct for 400yd (366m) without bayonet, and the second was correct for 600yd (549m) without bayonet. Besides, not all soldiers were the brightest material: 'In actual practice with men of little intelligence the flip-sight was something in the nature of a severe headache. Despite oft-repeated injunctions … one would always find some chap whose shots were going high say, at 200 yards [184m], the result of firing with his 600 yards [549m] battle-sight!'[44] Many rifles were manufactured with excess play in the aperture sights, which did not aid accuracy or confidence:

> Although the No. 4 rifle had for a year or two been the standard service arm of the British Forces … thousands of men, many of them old soldiers … regarded it as of small worth, and who swore by their SMLEs … and they never really bothered to try and shoot well with the No. 4. I had in my platoon an old soldier who, for some months after joining us, shot quite indifferently. When I tackled him he said he could never shoot with such a rifle, and wanted an SMLE. I allowed him to use my own SMLE one day, and he put up a really good score. I borrowed an SMLE which was fitted with a Parker-Hale aperture sight, and after imploring him to use the sight properly allowed him to fire the same practice as the day before. From then on he took kindly to the No. 4 [sights] and continued to shoot exceedingly well.[45]

Gradually the No. 4 began to filter into the hands of line regiments, who received it with mixed feelings. New weapons are always regarded with a certain amount of suspicion, particularly among the normally cynical front-line soldiers, but it gradually began to win some converts:

British soldiers in Burma. The man on the left holds an SMLE of indeterminate vintage, while the soldier on the right carries an up-to-date No. 4. Both models served alongside each other throughout the war. (IWM SE 2138)

It was a handy rifle, quite light and easy to point and aim quickly. I thought it accurate, but I was always a good shot. It was certainly effective at longer ranges, when I became a sniper I could shoot it quite well at 1,000 yards [914m]. It was certainly very good at four or five hundred yards [366–457m] with the rearsight properly set.[46]

Some of the earliest action involving the No. 4 was in Italy. When Private Jim Richardson landed with Eighth Army on 3 September 1943, he had no idea he would be fighting without a break for the next year and a half, during which time he carried his No. 4 continuously:

The winter [of 1943] was terrible and we were stuck on the German lines up in the mountains. We couldn't wash or shave and there was little in the way of hot food. Our rifles froze up, we had no oil and even if we had, it was too cold to have been much use. We took to carrying our bolts inside our battledress to keep them warm and when we were on sentry I prayed no bloody Jerries would attack because we'd have had to use our bayonets.[47]

Such an issue was not the fault of the Lee-Enfield itself, for all weapons suffered in the bitter cold – Vickers guns had to be emptied of their coolant and their locks kept warm; even revolvers jammed because of frozen mud and water. Private Richardson wrapped himself and his rifle in blankets in an attempt to keep both warm, but it was thanks to the timely intervention of soldiers serving with the Polish Brigade that the Army was able to keep its weapons functioning: 'They said to mix oil with petrol and keep our rifles lubricated with it. Apparently it worked on the Russian Front, so the QM [quartermaster] took a load of jerricans and mixed old engine oil with petrol and it did seem to work OK. I did hear that even the Service Corps were doing it to the engines in the trucks to keep them working.'[48]

In the jungles of Burma, the Chindits, formed by Major-General Orde Wingate, began fighting the Japanese in February 1943 and cold weather was the least of their problems. Officially they carried Bren guns, Vickers medium machine guns and Enfield No. 1 Mk IIIs. Unofficially they took with them any weapons that they believed were suitable for the tough climatic conditions, including Thompson submachine guns, M1 carbines and during their later operations in March 1944, the No. 5 jungle carbine. Private T.J. Richards, who served with 5th Sherwood Foresters, recalled:

The carbine was powerful, I would say that for it, but it kicked like a mule and in jungle fighting it was slow to shoot. I had one for a while but gave it to one of our [Burmese] guides when I had the chance to get hold of an American M1 carbine. That was lovely, it was light and being semi-automatic was much better at close-quarter fighting. I'm not sure many of the blokes kept their Enfields, it was not a good soldier's rifle.[49]

If it wasn't ideal as an infantry rifle, one little-known facility of the No. 5 was its very efficient use as a grenade launcher:

One interesting point about the No. 5 is that it can be used as a light mortar, hurling grenades a distance of about 250 yards [229m]. When used in this role the launcher is attached to the flash eliminator and a mortar sight fastened just above the breech. A second rubber pad is slipped over the butt. For high angle fire the butt is placed on the ground ... low angle fire takes place from the shoulder, and up to ten grenades can be fired without undue discomfort.[50]

Used in this role, the rifle pre-empted the much later adoption of grenade tubes mounted underneath service assault rifles, such as the 40mm M203 for the M16 and GP30 for the AK-47.

As the Allied forces fought their way across Europe, British and Commonwealth snipers, having undertaken rigorous training, at last began to see what their Lee-Enfield rifles were capable of. Fighting through the dense Normandy bocage country was slow and tough, and most sniping was done at relatively close ranges. Sniper Sergeant Harry Furness of The York & Lancaster Regiment recalled shooting his first German at a range of less than 50yd (46m), so close that his telescopic sight was useless, but he was able to bring up, aim and snap-shoot the compact rifle very quickly.

Normally, however, sniper combat was much more a war of patience and nerve, and with the No. 4 (T) and the excellent optics of the No. 32 scope the British snipers had one of the best weapons of its type on the battlefield. For two days two snipers of The Cambridge Regiment waited to spot a German sniper who had shot their officer. On the afternoon of the third day, they finally had some luck:

A Black Watch sniper with a No. 4 (T) watches for potential targets. He is resting the muzzle of his rifle on a balustrade to steady it, but no sniper would risk shooting from such a position unless he was very sure enemy snipers were not in the vicinity. (IWM B 14626)

'Here, come and have a look.'

Packham grabbed his rifle. Without stirring so much as a leaf of their protective screen he slipped his rifle through the furrow. Removing the leather [lens] cap he stared through the telescopic lens.

'Can't see a thing,' he said, two minutes later. 'What am I looking for?'

'Smoke,' was the laconic reply. 'The bastard's having a fag.'

'Who's going to have him?' Packham queried, softly.

'You fire,' Arthur replied. 'I'll watch and make sure you get him.'

Although they had identified his hide, the German evaded them. The next morning they were in position well before dawn.

The German must have overslept for he was late getting into position. At 6.10 precisely his head and shoulders appeared for a second or two framed in an archway of foliage. Packham fired a single shot. All that Arthur saw was the German's rifle pirouetting in the sky.

'Got him,' he said with satisfaction.[51]

As the fighting moved across Europe, conditions varied greatly, from mountains in Italy to the flat pastoral landscape of Holland and western Germany. The open spaces and scattered villages frequently required shooting at ranges in excess of 500yd (457m) and while this was normally beyond the abilities of an ordinary rifleman, the scopes of the No. 4 (T) rifles made it quite feasible, often to the surprise of those concerned:

Another day in the same sector I picked up with my telescope a whole bunch of Huns about 700 yards [640m] away, digging like mad. The Americans ... had no intention of doing anything about them. Anyhow we decided to have a crack at them, much to our American comrades' amusement and amazement. We fired from a position in a house and hit at least two Jerries in the day. We missed a couple too ... but the expression of utter surprise on their faces as I saw it through my telescope at being sniped from 700 yards away was something I shall always remember.[52]

North Burma, 1944 (opposite)

Chindits of 77th Indian Brigade stalk the enemy through dense jungle. The point man is holding his Lee-Enfield No. 4 rifle, but it was quickly realized that long-barrelled bolt-action rifles such as the No. 4 were of questionable value in the jungle, where ambush, or dealing with tree-based snipers, required a quick response and a high rate of return fire. The second soldier cradles a No. 5 Mk I jungle carbine. In an environment where every pound of additional weight carried drained a soldier's energy reserves, the short-barrelled No. 5 was less tiring to carry through jungle and easier to shoulder and fire quickly than previous Lee-Enfields, but it was always an unhappy compromise. 9mm submachine guns, normally ideal for close combat, simply did not have the bullet weight to punch through dense foliage, and the Commonwealth forces lacked a rifle-calibre selective-fire weapon such as the US .30in Browning Automatic Rifle (BAR). As a result, the addition of a Bren gunner to patrols was regarded as vitally important.

Salvaged rifles being examined by a Royal Electrical and Mechanical Engineers (REME) armourer. These are a mixture of SMLEs and No. 4s, and those deemed worth repair would be overhauled by the unit armourers. Badly damaged weapons were robbed for parts and scrapped. (IWM B 14326)

The much-detested spike bayonet on a No. 4. It was actually an efficient tool for its intended purpose, and its fixing method was particularly strong, but soldiers disliked the fact that it could not be used for anything else, as it had no cutting edge. (Bob Maze)

Fighting in Europe after D-Day was made particularly difficult because of the abundance of rain that fell, and as their fathers had discovered in the trenches of France and Flanders, soldiers found that keeping a rifle functioning in such conditions was hard work. 'I used to clean my rifle every night, and oil the barrel and bolt. It was never left in the open, but in the morning, because of the incessant wet conditions, it would have begun rusting. Keeping the scope dry was also very difficult, moisture got in and fogged the lenses and it was a constant battle to make sure everything worked properly.'[53]

Under normal circumstances, however, looking after the rifles was relatively straightforward; they field-stripped easily for cleaning, although losing the bolt or bolt-head was fraught with problems, as head-spacing for the cartridge was critical. A replacement bolt or bolt-head could not simply be retrofitted, and required the services of the unit armourer. This had always been a matter that affected Lee-Enfields in general and was not unique to the No. 4. If there was any criticism it was reserved for the new spike bayonet. Whereas the old Pattern 1907 bayonet had been regarded as too long and unwieldy, the opposite applied to the No. 4 Mk I or 'pig sticker', as it was unflatteringly called. 'It was a bloody useless wee thing, about the only thing it was good for was knocking a couple of holes in a tin of condensed milk. You couldn't even open a can with it.'[54] It did prove practical as a probe for detecting mines, but as a general combat bayonet it was pretty hopeless, and while variants were introduced to try to create something more practical, it was not successfully replaced until the adoption of the FN/FAL and its knife bayonet.

THE END OF THE LINE

After 1945 the assorted patterns of Lee-Enfields in service were returned to store. The now-venerable SMLEs were mostly refurbished, sorted and sold off to colonial or Third World buyers, whilst the No. 4s were retained for use. The thorny question of replacement begun before the war had ended, but despite trials, no consensus had been reached so the cessation of hostilities did not mean an immediate end for the Lee-Enfield.

British and Commonwealth soldiers continued to carry it in a number of small-scale wars such as Suez (1956) and the Malayan Emergency (1948–60), but its greatest post-war use was during the Korean War (1950–53). For the British troops sent to fight on the 38th Parallel, the conditions would prove to be harder than anything many had faced in Europe. Mountainous regions, open hills exposed to biting sub-zero winds and heavy rain rapidly showed up any inadequacies in weapons and equipment. If many soldiers found that they were under-dressed for the prevailing winter temperatures, generally there were few complaints about their Lee-Enfields, which stood up well to the rigours of the campaign.

In what was destined to become the largest combat action since World War II, the British 29th Infantry Brigade faced a massive assault on the Imjin River (22–25 April 1951). During the savage fighting, 1st Battalion, The Gloucestershire Regiment, withdrew to a defensive position known as Hill 235, where for two days they held out against massed enemy infantry attacks. While their Vickers guns helped materially in cutting swathes through the attackers, the men of the rifle companies fired their No. 4 rifles until they were too hot to touch and the bolts became stiff and unworkable. Rifles were picked up from the dead and wounded.

Little had changed in terms of infantry small arms when the Korean War broke out in 1950. Here two Australians occupy a foxhole, the nearest holding an SMLE Mk III. These were manufactured in Australia throughout World War II at seven separate sites. The No. 4 rifle was not made in Australia. (Australian War Memorial)

Men fired continuously at the advancing hordes, but as fast as they shot them down, they were replaced by a seemingly inexhaustible supply of enemy soldiers. So densely packed were the Koreans that a single bullet would bring down two or three men, but it mattered little. When the artillery could no longer provide support, the Glosters commander had little option but to order his men to make their way back to the British lines as best they could.[55]

The British brigade lost a total of 1,091 men, the Glosters sustaining 621 men killed, wounded or missing. However, their opponents suffered some 10,000 men killed or wounded during the attack – the North Korean Sixty-Third Army comprised 27,000 fighting troops before this engagement, and they were subsequently withdrawn from combat. Many of the Korean dead and wounded, in echoes of 1914, were hit as a result of the accurate rifle fire laid down.

Although the matter needed little reinforcing, in the wake of the conflict it was obvious to the Ministry of Defence and the Army generally that semi-automatic arms were far superior for combat use, particularly where long-distance shooting was not a prerequisite. For all that, the Army still had snipers, though admittedly not many. Those who served in Korea acquitted themselves well, despite the fact that they carried rifles that had already seen much service in World War II. The Australians were still carrying their SMLE Mk III sniping rifles in Korea, and often had to engage the enemy at the extreme range of their weapons. One Australian sniper, Ian Robertson, set himself up to shoot at a track that was much used by Korean soldiers. However, it was beyond the scope's maximum elevation setting of 1,000yd (914m), and Robertson had to use experience and a large amount of guesswork to work out where the bullets were hitting:

When they [Korean soldiers] had passed a particular point, if I fired then, they would run into the bullet. I tried an experimental shot low down and saw the blast of the bullet [hit] just above that bloke, so I made another guess and fired another shot and this bloke disappeared. It seemed to confirm what I thought. I kept doing this between other duties. All this went on for about a week. When we finally took the hill I thought 'I've got to go and have a look at this' ... there were about 30 bodies down there in front of the pit. I went a bit like jelly for a minute and thought 'Oh, shit. I'm in a grisly business here.'[56]

The Lee-Enfield continued in the guise of the L42 sniping rifle, a variant of the L8 rifle. Visually it differed from the old weapon by means of its distinctive lack of forend woodwork. This image shows an SAS soldier cradling an L42. He has a US M79 grenade launcher on his backpack. (Author)

Despite the fact that he was shooting a rifle designed almost 50 years earlier, Robertson's experiences show that the Enfield design clearly had life left in it. Surprisingly, Australia had continued to manufacture the No. 1 Mk III SMLE throughout World War II and a sniper variant, the No. 1 Mk III* HT with Pattern 1918 scope, served with the Australians through Korea until it and all other bolt-action rifles were replaced by the semi-automatic FN/FAL.

Progress could not be halted, however, and the Enfield was eventually withdrawn from British and Commonwealth service in 1957, when the FN/FAL was introduced. The Ministry of Defence soon realised that there was a fundamental problem in adopting the new semi-automatic rifle, for there was no available sniping variant. In fact, its construction, with a sheet-steel receiver, made it very difficult to be adapted for an optical sight, so the MoD decision-makers were faced with two solutions: either opt for the lengthy and potentially expensive course of finding, trialling and adopting a brand-new sniping rifle, or upgrade the existing one. There was no denying that the Enfield was now old technology, but in view of the excellent accuracy achieved when testing the 7.62mm L8, it was decided to opt for the latter course.

As a result, the last Enfield-pattern rifle was approved for service on 24 August 1970. The L42A1 with Telescope L1A1 was really no more than an improved No. 4 (T) rifle. The work undertaken was basic: a heavy 7.62mm barrel with a 1-in-12 right-hand twist was fitted, as was a new bolt-head marked with '19T' (the pressure generated by the new cartridge). The forend woodwork was completely dispensed with and an improved No. 32 Mk III scope was fitted. These were World War II-production scopes, but were totally overhauled, with new lenses, range drums and improved waterproofing. Despite misgivings about the ability of a basically obsolete rifle to meet the expected performance criteria, the L42 proved itself a very effective sniping rifle, with a performance capability well beyond that for which it was designed.

The L42's performance was proven very effectively in Northern Ireland in 1972, when two L42-armed observing snipers (unusually, one was an officer) saw a Ferret armoured car blown up by a mine. IRA men began to arrive, putting the crew of the Ferret in a perilous situation. The snipers decided to act, and between them shot ten IRA men. The furthest target hit was an astounding 1,408yd (1,287m) away but no one at Brigade HQ could believe the ranges involved, so demanded by radio – while the engagement was in full flow – to know what type of weapons were being used.

During the Falklands War (April–June 1982), once again the venerable L42s saw hard use. Here the deficiencies of the old bolt-action design came to the fore, as many snipers, having run out of oil and cleaning materials, found they were unable to keep their rifles functioning in the salt-laden air of the islands. Conditions were reminiscent of the trenches of World War I, as bolts seized, bores rusted and cartridges mildewed. One sniper admitted abandoning his L42 in favour of an Argentinian FN/FAL, but not all snipers were prepared to go to such lengths, to the great relief of at

least one platoon of 2nd Battalion, The Parachute Regiment. From seemingly out of nowhere, they came under sniper fire:

> A bullet shot past my face. It was so close I felt it physically. All of us automatically dived to the ground.
>
> Someone called out, 'It's a f*****g sniper.'
>
> To our rear I noticed a bush. Not that surprising, we were in a field, but this bush was different, it was moving. It became apparent that it was not a bush but a member of our Sniper Platoon. He jumped up on top of the wall. Two more rapid shots flew over. The bush remained on the wall and from under one of his branches pulled out a pair of binoculars.
>
> 'Definitely a sniper,' declared the bush … and with that he finally jumped down off the wall and crawled off to our right. After about twenty metres [22yd] he stopped, aimed his rifle and fired a single shot.
>
> 'Think I got him,' said the bush.
>
> After the battle, the British bush had gone in search of the Argentinian bush. On finding him he discovered that he had shot him clean through the head at a distance of over 1,000 metres [1,093yd].[57]

But the Falklands was to be the swansong of the Enfield, for late in 1982 the Army's new sniping rifle, the L96A1, was introduced, and the L42s, the last remnants of the Enfield dynasty, were handed in for indefinite storage. It was a fitting end for a truly venerable rifle.

LEE-ENFIELDS AROUND THE WORLD

A quick count by the author of countries that officially adopted the Lee-Enfield has come to 46, not including the United Kingdom, although even this figure could doubtless be enlarged upon. Sales figures have always been a good indicator of the success of a specific design (it is noteworthy that no other country, aside from Jamaica, Bolivia and Nepal, has ever adopted the SA80/L85A1, for example).

Aden, 1964 (previous pages)

A Royal Marine sniper patrol has taken up position in a 'sangar' in the Kurhbar Pass region of Aden. The observer (also a trained sniper) is armed with a 9mm L2A1 Sterling submachine gun for close protection, and he watches for enemy activity through a 20× Scout Regiment spotting scope. The sniper tracks a possible target using the No. 32 Mk II scope mounted on a World War II-vintage .303in Lee-Enfield No. 4 (T) sniping rifle. Although the .303in was by this date an obsolete calibre, little thought had been given to replacing Britain's ageing No. 4 (T) rifles, so the Lee-Enfield soldiered on as Britain's front-line sniping rifle until replaced by the 7.62mm L42A1 rifle in 1970. In marked contrast to the Lee-Enfield, the NCO on the right has his 7.62mm L1A1 Self-Loading Rifle (the British version of the FN/FAL) propped up next to him. Adopted in 1954, it proved a reliable combat weapon, but it was extremely difficult to mount the weapon with a telescopic sight, and it lacked the long-range shooting ability of the Lee-Enfield.

Owning and shooting the Lee-Enfield

Over many years the author has owned and has shot all of the Enfield models. The overwhelming feeling that these rifles have is one of solid build quality and dependability. While this is as much in the mind as in the hands, never in 30 years has the author shot an Enfield that had proved troublesome – poor-quality ammunition aside. Early models, such as the Lee-Metfords and Long Lees, are certainly quite cumbersome to handle, although no worse than comparable rifles then in service; their sighting leaves something to be desired, but on a target range they prove accurate and all have remarkably crisp trigger actions, sadly lacking on the later models. The SMLE is undoubtedly easier to handle than the long rifles, and despite early criticisms of its sighting arrangements, the rearsight mounted in front of the breech does not seem to be any hindrance to aiming. Accuracy for a rifle with a new bore was officially 2½ MOA at 100yd (2.5in/64mm at 91m). With military-issue ball this performance was perfectly feasible and a good shot could normally reduce it to 1½ MOA.

Using hand-loaded ammunition, on one (memorably rare) occasion the author managed to shoot the centre out of a bull at 300yd (274m) with ten shots, firing a scoped Trials No. 4 (T) rifle of 1931 vintage. Other shooters can do better, and not for nothing is the No. 4 (T) still a very sought-after rifle for modern 'sniping' competitions. Any sort of mechanical failure is rare, but the locking system of the bolts (slightly less strong than that of the Mauser system) does mean that over time they stretch, so head-spacing is critical. Bolt action is smooth and the bolt handle certainly aids quick reloading, thus raising the rate of fire. Most magazines now are well bedded in and rarely cause problems. There are sufficient Lee-Enfields about to ensure a ready supply for years to come, indeed thousands have just appeared from storage in Nepal, and doubtless many hundreds more will surface likewise. Although their military service is finished, they will be around for decades to come.

Some unexpected countries have used the Enfield: the United States was supplied with large numbers when the American Expeditionary Forces (AEF) entered World War I, mainly because of ammunition supply problems with the .30in Springfields that they carried. Many photographs exist of AEF soldiers with SMLEs, although some firearms enthusiasts still refuse to accept that this was ever the case. From sketchy reports that have survived, it appeared that the Enfield was well liked for its compact size, but was not regarded as being as accurate or powerful as the Mauser-based M1903 Springfield, chambered for the .30-06 cartridge. Turkey captured large numbers of SMLEs from Australian and New Zealand Army Corps (ANZAC) and British forces after 1915 and these were converted to use 7.92mm Mauser ammunition, although how effective this conversion was remains unknown, as examples are very rare today.

During World War II tens of thousands of No. 4s and SMLEs were dropped into occupied territory for use by Resistance units, particularly in France, Holland and Norway. In France today (where the author lives) nice examples regularly turn up, having languished in barns and cellars for decades. Free French forces were issued with the No. 4 for the invasion of France in June 1944. This distribution was apparently much to General de Gaulle's displeasure, as he wanted French soldiers to be carrying French weapons, but alas for him, there were none to be had.

At first glance, this is not a particularly remarkable photograph, but these soldiers are in the American Expeditionary Forces and the man at the right has his carefully wrapped SMLE on the ground. Shortages of .30-06 ammunition for the Springfield rifle resulted in many American units being supplied with SMLEs. (NARA)

Around the world paramilitary and police units still carry Lee-Enfields of all vintages, as do insurgent groups. In the early 21st century, this late World War I-production SMLE was photographed still providing good service for Maoist rebels in Nepal. (Jonathan Alpeyrie)

Naturally, countries such as India and post-Partition Pakistan and Bangladesh used locally manufactured Enfields, of both SMLE and No. 4 patterns. Between 1905 and the mid-1970s tens of thousands were made in the Indian Armaments Factory at Ishapore in Bengal, and from 1957 No. 4 rifles were made at the Pakistan Ordnance Factory in Wah. Many rural-based Pakistani policemen can still be seen carrying these rifles, which do not yet appear to have been totally replaced by the military-issue Heckler & Koch G3 assault rifle.

Although the ubiquitous AK-47 is now the most widely manufactured and most-carried small arm in history (current estimates of its production numbers run to 100 million), Enfields still turn up regularly in the hands of dissident groups, terrorists and insurgents, as well as the police and militia of Third World countries. One British ex-soldier who took part in a raid in Afghanistan in 2009 told the author that among a cache of RPG rockets, AK-47 ammunition and explosives, they found half a dozen SMLE rifles. Clearly, in many countries throughout the world, the end of the Lee-Enfield's useful life has not yet been reached.

An Afghan fighter holds his Lee-Enfield up for the photographer. Judging by his apparently satisfied expression, the old rifle appears to meet all his needs. (Massoud Hossaini/AFP/Getty Images)

IMPACT
The Lee-Enfield legacy

What is the legacy of a rifle like the Lee-Enfield? After all, it was not initially a particularly innovative design and the choice of cartridge was in many ways a surprising one. As we have seen, when first introduced the rifle was subject to a barrage of complaints from those who regarded the old single-shot design of the Martini-Henry as irreplaceable. By the late 1870s, however, the Martini-Henry was no longer a viable weapon for a modern army. British military doctrine still relied on tactics such as the defensive square, or linear warfare with two or three lines of soldiers using volley fire. It harked back to the days of Waterloo and a thin red line of smoking muskets, but as the 20th century approached such tactics had become outmoded and dangerous. This new reality was sharply underlined by losses sustained by the British soldiers in battles such as that at Isandlwana (22 January 1879), in which more than 1,300 British troops were killed by an overwhelming force of Zulu warriors. The reliability of the Martini-Henry was seriously outweighed by its slowness to load and fire, and range limitations.

In the world of weapons technology, the introduction of the magazine rifle was both innovative and very effective. One of its earliest incarnations was invented by an American, Christopher Spencer, in 1860. It chambered a .56in rimfire cartridge and was loaded from a tube magazine in the butt by means of a lever action, which inserted the cartridge as well as cocking the action. The Spencer was the first repeating arm to enter military service, but it was simply a matter of time before similar systems were adopted, in some form or other, by almost every other major power. In many respects, the first Enfields were the result not of innovative British arms technology, but of American, German and Swiss design. That is not to decry the Enfield, for few inventions are the result of one single idea or one individual's thought processes. Normally they are the logical conclusion to a lengthy progression of ideas and experiments, some successful, many not.

Britain, having watched international rifle development from the sidelines for some years, eventually felt it could not prevaricate any more. It was fortunate that by the time British decision-makers decided that a new weapon was required, there were several good rifles already on the market from which they could pick and choose the most important aspects, and ensure that their eventual decision would prove to be a sound one. That the wind of change was blowing very fast indeed is witnessed by the fact that by the time the first Enfield trials models were introduced in 1888, black-powder ammunition was already out of date. The new generation of bolt-action rifles was an advance in weapons technology as important as the introduction of the Minié rifle had been four decades before. Then, few military men appreciated that this simple ballistic advance had effectively shifted the parameters of warfare; the age of the cavalry charge and massed infantry attacks was now past in the face of aimed fire from 500yd (457m) or beyond.

Initially the natives who faced these new weapons were incapable of opposing them, and Britain's successes in colonial wars led the British to believe that their Army was indeed superior to any other. It was not until the dawn of the 20th century, when they were faced by an opponent on a level playing field, that it began to dawn on the Army that this was not entirely the case. When British soldiers were met by the accurate rifle fire of the Boers, the world of colonial warfare was turned on its head. For the first time, the Army of Her Britannic Majesty was facing an opponent armed with equal technology, superior tactics and a better grasp of the type of warfare involved. That the Lee-Metfords and Lee-Enfields were some of the best rifles on the battlefield was indisputable, but the shortcomings in training men to use them properly were glaring. As with the issue of the first rifled muskets 40 years previously, it was the case that soldiers simply did not have the training to enable them to take advantage of the technology they were equipped with. The British Enfields and the Boers' Mausers, Krags, Mannlichers, etc., were certainly cutting edge, but in reality only the army that knew how to use them properly held any real advantage.

Thus it appeared, in its early days at least, that the introduction of the Enfield rifle provided the Army with little or no material benefit. Certainly, the ability of the soldier to shoot further and with greater accuracy was unquestionable, but if the enemy could do this as well, where did the advantage lie? The war in South Africa was a salutary lesson for the British Army and lessons had to be learned. These lessons took the form of modifying the service rifle and improving the training for the men issued with it, for one without the other was pointless. Teaching the men to estimate distances and understand their rifles was comparatively straightforward; even though the Army was still uneasy about the concept, it was a major leap forwards.

Improving the rifle was not so simple, but the designers and engineers at Enfield rose to the task and their eventual production of the first Short Rifle in 1902 was a concept that was nothing short of groundbreaking. The significance of this event is difficult to comprehend today, but it should be remembered that until the introduction of the SMLE, armies had been forced to issue two or even three types of rifle to different branches of the services. In Britain, the Royal Navy traditionally had its own short rifles, while the Army's mounted units and artillery had carbines and the infantry were armed with long rifles. Such diversity placed a huge burden on the factories responsible for small-arms manufacture, as well as creating supply and spares problems. There was, too, the important consideration of cost, for carbines were as labour-intensive to make as any other long-arm.

Yet, at a stroke, the British government managed to dispense with all of these problems by adopting, in the face of fierce criticism, a rifle that was – by the standards of the day – radical.

British soldiers with fixed bayonets advance through the desert dust during the battle for Nufilia in Libya, 1943. Keeping rifles clean in such conditions was a serious problem, as the talcum-like dust clogged all mechanical parts. Small arms worked best when no lubricants at all were used. (IWM E 20501)

Despite comments in the press that the Short Rifle was 'neither fish nor fowl' and would 'fail woefully in its task', the arm was to set a new benchmark in weapon design, in part because until well into the Victorian era much rifle development in Britain had been unduly influenced by the requirements of target shooters. After the Second Boer War, some senior officers began to appreciate that there was now a widening gulf between the requirements of the soldier and civilian, and the introduction of the SMLE reinforced this. An anonymous writer in *The Times* newspaper in 1907 put his finger on the most obvious fact of modern warfare, namely that a rifle suitable for the 1,000yd target range was now no longer suitable for the battlefield:

> This controversy relates to the whole value as a military exercise of encouraging competition in which prizes are awarded for the skill in hitting a target. It is deemed by many that the continued inculcation among trained soldiers [scoring bull's eyes] is [a] very unsound tactical idea but is also in no way a preparation for engaging the targets that will be found on active service. A high level of rapid fire and accuracy in snap-shooting is required … and for this purpose a high number of trustworthy shots are of far more value than a few marksmen. But from the above it must not be inferred for one moment that the short rifle is not a good shooting weapon. On the contrary, so far from being the case, it is an excellent one.[58]

The use of the very latest manufacturing technology, allied to clever design on the part of the Enfield engineers, made such a rifle possible. The realization dawned that the older long rifles were actually of no material benefit to the soldier, because the nature of warfare had changed. It could even be argued that the SMLE was the first tentative step on the road to the adoption of the modern assault rifle.

CONCLUSION

The introduction of the SMLE broke all of the rules of European arms design and in doing so forced the British Army to re-think its own strategy and training. That they took this seriously is evidenced in the new system of musketry that was adopted and the subsequent very effective application of it in the opening stages of World War I. The rapid fire from the BEF's rifles often denuded the battlefield of German soldiers so utterly that one soldier commented that '… it looked as though a scythe had cut across it, for there was nothing left standing, save the occasional arm of a wounded man waving helplessly'.[59] If there were doubters, here was proof positive that in properly trained hands, there was nothing at all wrong with the concept of a short-barrelled rifle for general military issue. The impact of these rifles was also reflected in the eventual adoption of short rifles by all major combat powers. The USA had looked with interest on the debate, and also decided on a short rifle, the Springfield Model 1903. In Germany, increasingly large numbers of the shortened variant of the Gew 98 rifle, the Kar 98, were introduced in 1908; by the end of the war the Kar 98 had become extremely popular with infantry units, who found the long rifle too awkward and heavy, and some 1.5 million are believed to have been manufactured.[60] This rifle metamorphosed into the standard-issue Kar 98k carried throughout World War II by Axis soldiers.

While it cannot be claimed that the Lee-Enfield was solely responsible for this change, it is certainly true that the introduction of the SMLE, with its unconventional design, had a pronounced effect on military thinking. After the cessation of hostilities in 1918, when Britain re-evaluated its small arms, it was clear that there could be little gained in deviating from the path it had taken with making service rifles smaller and lighter. The abortive experiments in 1913 with the .276in cartridge had shown that good performance could be obtained without resorting to large calibres, and had World War I not intervened, undoubtedly Britain would have adopted the smaller cartridge and the Pattern 1914 rifle to go with it.

After World War II, experiments began with a similar calibre, the .280in, and the EM-1/2 assault rifle. That it was not adopted was shameful, but the RSAF at Enfield was at least able to continue in its role of supplying the British Army with rifles, initially taking on manufacture of the L1A1 SLR (the British version of the FN/FAL) in 1954, then the SA80/L85 assault rifle from 1986. Times had changed, though, and problems with the SA80 made its continued manufacture uneconomical; besides, the RSAF site had by then become a valuable piece of real estate. The privatization of RSAF (becoming Royal Ordnance) coincided with the closure of the old Enfield Lock factory in August 1987. Ironically, the German firm of Heckler & Koch, a subsidiary of Royal Ordnance, was then contracted to upgrade the L85 and provide spare parts. Exactly who will manufacture the next generation of rifles for the British Army is unclear, but it seems that, for the first time in 400 years, it will not be a UK-based company.

The fine traditions of craftsmanship and quality that the RSAF provided were based on the old methods of gunmaking, and these sufficed until the end of World War I. Many regard the pre-1916 SMLE as probably the last rifle to be made with a Victorian attitude to quality of manufacture. However, after 1916 times changed very fast for the firearms industry, and speed of production, allied to even tighter cost-efficiency, became the new watchwords. The No. 4 rifle was the last gasp of traditional military firearms manufacture in Britain. Post-war, mass-production controlled by accountants and utilizing contract-supplied components and highly automated assembly would be the new ways forward. Given sufficient investment, RSAF Enfield could possibly have competed in this new world, but skilled workers were now too expensive and in peacetime there was no longer the budget to pay for them. Since 1816, they had been producing the finest rifles that money could buy and these weapons enabled the British Army to control the most lucrative empire in history, as well as carry Britain through the two world wars. Alas, Enfield and its associated firearms were very much a product of their times and for better or worse, those times have now gone.

No. 4 rifles being assembled at the Long Branch factory in Toronto, Canada. These rifles were built to the same high specifications as Enfield-produced weapons, and often the quality of stocking was better as there was a greater selection of wood available. The open butt trap, for holding the pull-through and oil bottle, is clearly visible here. (Long Branch official photograph)

75

GLOSSARY

APERTURE SIGHT: A micro-adjustable rearsight with tiny viewing aperture that provides the shooter with a sharp target image.

BATTLESIGHT: A simple one- or two-position fixed rearsight for shooting at short ranges.

BEDDING: The method by which the barrel and receiver are fixed rigidly into the stock.

BOAT-TAIL: A bullet with a tapered rear section that helps streamline it for flight.

BOLT: The mechanism that closes the breech for firing and contains the firing pin.

BOLT HANDLE: The protruding handle that enables the bolt to be opened and closed.

BREECH: The rear of the barrel that contains the chamber into which the cartridge is inserted.

CHARGER-LOADING: Aka clip-loading. The use of a pre-loaded sprung-metal clip to insert cartridges into the magazine, normally five at a time.

CUT-OFF: A metal plate designed to slide across the lower part of the receiver, isolating the magazine.

EJECTION: The action of the extractor removing and throwing away the fired cartridge case.

EXTRACTOR: A small hooked metal bar on the face of the bolt that pulls the cartridge out of the breech.

FREE-FLOATING: Mounting a barrel to ensure no part of it touches the stock beyond the breech.

MAGAZINE: The ammunition feed system for a rifle. It may take the form of a removable box (e.g. Lee-Enfield), an internal magazine (e.g. Mauser) or a tube underneath the barrel (e.g. Winchester).

RECEIVER: The body of a rifle that contains the bolt and usually the magazine.

RIMLESS CARTRIDGE: Ammunition in which the base rim is the same diameter as the cartridge wall at the base (e.g. 7.92mm).

RIMMED CARTRIDGE: Ammunition that features a projecting rim around the base of the cartridge, the rim being of greater diameter than the case wall (e.g. .303in).

SLING SWIVEL: Metal loops on the stock through which a leather or webbing sling is passed for carrying or to steady the rifle for shooting.

SPITZER: A pointed-nose bullet.

REFERENCES

[1] SAC Progress Report, January 1887, in *Small Arms Committee Minutes and Reports 1876-1899* (n.d.)

[2] *Small Arms Committee Minutes and Reports 1876–1899* (n.d.)

[3] Ibid.

[4] Ibid.

[5] Ibid.

[6] British Patent J.P. Lee No. 11319, 18 August 1887

[7] British Patent J.J. Speed No. 6335, 30 April 1887

[8] Extracted from *The Evening Post*, 13 August 1887

[9] *The Times*, 12 September 1889

[10] *Small Arms Committee Minutes and Reports 1900–1939* (n.d.)

[11] G. Coppard, *With a Machine Gun to Cambrai* (1980)

[12] G.H. Frost (ed.), *Munitions of War, a Record of the BSA Company, 1914–1918* (n.d.)

[13] I. Skennerton, *The Lee Enfield Story* (1993). Skennerton lists 173 contractors

[14] *Statistics of the Military Effort of the British Empire 1914–1918* (1922)

[15] Figure from I. Skennerton, *The British Sniper* (1984). This figure is now regarded as on the low side, as examples produced by previously unrecorded makers are coming to light

[16] Corporal T. Durst, personal interview

[17] H.V. Hesketh-Prichard, *Sniping in France* (1994)

[18] Durst, op. cit.

[19] *Small Arms Committee Minutes and Reports 1900–1939*

[20] Captain C. Shore, *With British Snipers to the Reich* (1948)

[21] Ibid.

[22] *The Times*, 19 April 1896

[23] *The Times*, 25 April 1896

[24] Ibid.

[25] W.S. Churchill, *The River War* (1899)

[26] Ibid.

[27] F.M. Crum, *With the Mounted Infantry in South Africa* (1903)

[28] Ibid.

[29] H.C. Hillegas, *With The Boer Forces* (1900)

[30] D. Reitz, *Commando* (1929)

[31] *The Times*, 3 February 1905

[32] *The Times*, 25 February 1905, letter from Capt E.D. Johnson of The Rifle Brigade

[33] Hansard, Territorial Force Reserve Debate. *HL Deb, 28 July 1909, vol. 2*, cc. 799–804

[34] F. Richards, *Old Soldiers Never Die* (1936). His real name was Francis Philip Woodruff (1883–1961)

[35] Ibid.

[36] Ibid.

[37] Hesketh-Prichard, op. cit.

[38] Private F. Mowbray, personal interview

[39] Private C. Jarman, personal interview

[40] Major B. Penberthy, *Notes to Snipers* (1916)

[41] Sir J. Hammerton (ed.), *I Was There, Vol. 2* (1938–39); an anonymous Australian contributor

[42] Private W. Smith, personal interview

[43] Shore, op. cit.

[44] Ibid.

[45] Ibid.

[46] Sergeant H. Furness, correspondence with the author

[47] J. Richardson, *Italy and Beyond*, unpublished memoir

[48] T.J. Richards, correspondence with the author

[49] T.M. Spencer, correspondence with the author

[50] Shore, op. cit.

[51] B. Wynne, *Sniper* (1968). The biography of Private A. Hare, The Cambridge Regiment

[52] Shore, op. cit.

[53] Furness, op. cit.

[54] Smith, op. cit.

[55] M. Hastings, *The Korean War* (1987)

[56] Interview with Ian Robertson, 3rd Battalion, Royal Australian Regiment, *American Rifleman*, August 2003

[57] K. Lukowiak, *A Soldier's Song* (2000)

[58] *The Times*, 26 November 1907

[59] Sir J. Hammerton, ed., *I Was There, Vol. 1* (1938). An anonymous account of the battle of Mons

[60] J. Walters, *The German Rifle* (1979)

SELECT BIBLIOGRAPHY

Books and articles

Churchill, W.S., *The River War: An Historical Account of The Re-Conquest of the Soudan*, 2 vols, Longmans, Green & Co., London (1899)

Coppard, G., *With a Machine Gun to Cambrai*, Imperial War Museum, London (1980)

Crum, F.M., *With the Mounted Infantry in South Africa: Being Side-Lights on the Boer Campaign, 1899–1902*, Macmillan & Bowes, Cambridge (1903)

Edwards, Maj J.T., *The Service Rifle and How to Use It*, Gale & Polden, London (1941)

Frost, G.H. (ed.), *Munitions of War, a Record of the BSA Company, 1914–1918*, Birmingham (n.d.)

Hammerton, Sir J. (ed.), *I Was There, Vol. 1*, Amalgamated Press, London (1938)

Hammerton, Sir J. (ed.), *I Was There, Vol. 2*, Amalgamated Press, London (1938–39)

Hastings, M., *The Korean War*, Michael Joseph, London (1987)

Hesketh-Prichard, H.V., *Sniping in France*, Leo Cooper, London (1994)

Hillegas, H.C., *With The Boer Forces*, Methuen, London (1900)

Hogg, I. & Weeks, J., *Military Small Arms of the 20th Century*, Arms & Armour Press, London (1993)

Lukowiak, K., *A Soldier's Song: True Stories from the Falklands*, Phoenix, London (2000)

Penberthy, Maj B., *Notes to Snipers*, privately printed (1916)

Petrillo, A.M., *The Lee-Enfield No. 1 Rifles*, Excalibur, Tucson, AZ (1990)

Petrillo, A.M., *The Lee Enfield No. 4 Rifles*, Excalibur, Tucson, AZ (1992)

Reitz, D., *Commando*, Faber & Faber, London (1929)

Reynolds, Maj E., *The Lee-Enfield Rifle*, H. Jenkins, London (1962)

Richards, F., *Old Soldiers Never Die*, Faber & Faber, London (1936)

Richardson, J., *Italy and Beyond*, unpublished memoir

Robertson, I., interview, 3rd Battalion, Royal Australian Regiment, *American Rifleman* (August 2003)

Shore, Capt C., *With British Snipers to the Reich*, Small Arms Press, London (1948)

Skennerton, I., *The British Sniper: British and Commonwealth Sniping and Equipments 1915–1983*, Ian Skennerton, Margate, Australia (1984)

Skennerton, I., *The Lee-Enfield Story*, Greenhill, London (1993)

Stratton, C.R., *The British Enfield Rifles,* Vols 1 and 2, North Cape Publications, Tustin, CA (2009)

Walters, J., *The German Rifle*, Arms & Armour Press, London (1979)

Wynne, B., *Sniper*, London, Macdonald (1968)

Interviews and personal correspondence

Durst, Cpl T., The King's Royal Rifle Corps, personal interview

Furness, Sgt H., The York and Lancaster Regiment, correspondence with the author

Jarman, Pte C., The Queen's (Royal West Surrey Regiment), personal interview

Mowbray, Pte F., The King's Royal Rifle Corps, personal interview. The author's wife's great-uncle

Smith, Pte W., Royal Army Service Corps and 51st Highland Division, personal interview

Spencer, T.M., correspondence with the author

Newspapers

The Evening Post, 13 August 1887
The Times, 12 September 1889
The Times, 19 April 1896
The Times, 25 April 1896
The Times, 3 February 1905
The Times, 25 February 1905
The Times, 26 November 1907

Official publications

Hansard, Territorial Force Reserve Debate, *HL Deb*, 28 July 1909, Vol. 2, cc. 799–804

List of Changes, 23 December 1902

List of Changes, 1 February 1918

Small Arms Committee Minutes and Reports 1876–1899, HMSO, London (n.d.)

Small Arms Committee Minutes and Reports 1900–1939, HMSO, London (n.d.)

Statistics of the Military Effort of the British Empire 1914–1918, The War Office, London (1922)

INDEX